Praise for *Lafayette in the Somewhat United States*

"[A] freewheeling history of the Revolutionary War . . . Vowell points out that Lafayette was for a time 'a national obsession.'"
—*The New Yorker*

"Vowell wanders through the history of the American Revolution and its immediate aftermath, using Lafayette's involvement in the war as a map, and bringing us all along in her perambulations. . . . Her prose sparkles."
—*The New York Times Book Review*

"[Vowell] takes an open and observant 'Hey, that's nuts' stance toward past and present, which results in a book that's informative, funny, and insightful."
—*TIME*

"Gilded with snark, buoyant on charm, Vowell's brand of history categorically refuses to take itself—or any of its subjects—too seriously. . . . At once light-footed and lighthearted, her histories are—dare I say it—fun. And Lafayette is no different. . . . Vowell emerges from the Revolutionary War with an unabashed smile on her face. I'd be surprised if her reader doesn't, too."
—*NPR*

"[Vowell] turns the dusty chronicle of American history into a lively mash-up and then, playing the history nerd, delivers her stories in her flat funny voice."
—*The National Book Review*

"Sarah Vowell turns her keen eye and droll wit to the American Revolution in her latest historical venture, *Lafayette in the Somewhat United States*. . . . Vowell, of course, doesn't just give us the highlights; she offers a portrait of [Lafayette] and his older contemporaries, with whom he found friendship, glory, and endless bickering."
—*Cosmopolitan*

"Vowell takes on American history as only she can, this time with the story of Frenchman the Marquis de Lafayette, a Revolutionary War hero."
—*USA Today*

"To impress the history buff at the table, read Vowell's (ever the expert in, really, everything) in-depth and irreverent account of George Washington's decorated general Lafayette, which also looks to our own political climate for context."
—*Marie Claire*

"Nobody recounts American history the way Sarah Vowell does, with irreverence and humor and quirky details—history and facts, but also entertainment. [*Lafayette in the Somewhat United States*] is about the friendship between George Washington and the Marquis de Lafayette, but in Vowell's inimitable style it is also firmly grounded in the present."   —Minneapolis *Star Tribune*

"If you ever wanted an insightful and entertaining look at the friendship between George Washington and his French aristocrat general Marquis de Lafayette, this book by Sarah Vowell . . . should be on your list."   —*Kansas City Star*

"Vowell's sort of the Quentin Tarantino of popular history: She weaves pop culture and real life into her narrative, breaking down the barriers that keep history buried in the past."
            —*Milwaukee Journal Sentinel*

"Here's one historian who is a born storyteller."
            —*The Philadelphia Inquirer*

"With laugh-out-loud humor and her characteristic snark, Vowell . . . makes this walk through history a walk in the park."
            —*The Washington Post*

"Lafayette is lucky he has Sarah Vowell in his court."
            —*New Republic*

"Vowell has mined American history for surprising and amusing insights into the heart of the nation."   —*Slate*

"[Vowell is] as good at giving facts as she is at making sure you'll retain them by telling the story in the most fascinating way possible."
            —*Paste*

LAFAYETTE

in the

SOMEWHAT
UNITED STATES

Sarah Vowell

RIVERHEAD BOOKS
New York

RIVERHEAD BOOKS
An imprint of Penguin Random House LLC
375 Hudson Street
New York, New York 10014

Copyright © 2015 by Sarah Vowell
Penguin supports copyright. Copyright fuels creativity, encourages diverse voices,
promotes free speech, and creates a vibrant culture. Thank you for buying an authorized
edition of this book and for complying with copyright laws by not reproducing,
scanning, or distributing any part of it in any form without permission. You are
supporting writers and allowing Penguin to continue to publish books for every reader.

The Library of Congress has catalogued the Riverhead hardcover edition as follows:

Vowell, Sarah, date.
Lafayette in the somewhat United States / Sarah Vowell.
p.   cm.
ISBN 9781594631740
1. Lafayette, Marie Joseph Paul Yves Roch Gilbert Du Motier, marquis de, 1757–
1834.   2. Lafayette, Marie Joseph Paul Yves Roch Gilbert Du Motier, marquis de,
1757–1834—Influence.   3. United States—History—Revolution, 1775–1783—
Participation, French.   4. Generals—France—Biography.   5. Statesmen—France—
Biography.   6. Generals—United States—Biography.   7. France—Politics and
government—1789–1900.   I. Title.
E207.L2V69   2015   2015024639
355.0092—dc23
[B]

First Riverhead hardcover edition: October 2015
First Riverhead trade paperback edition: October 2016
Riverhead trade paperback edition ISBN: 9780399573101

Printed in the United States of America
1   3   5   7   9   10   8   6   4   2

Book design by Lauren Kolm

Illustrations by Teddy Newton

TO STEVEN BARCLAY, ALLY AND FRIEND

This continent is a vast, unwieldy machine.

—John Adams, 1775

We are not to expect to be translated from despotism
to liberty in a feather-bed.

—Thomas Jefferson to Lafayette, 1790

The country is behind you, fifty percent.

—Bob Hope, to United States troops in Vietnam, 1966

How did the Marquis de Lafayette win over the stingiest, crankiest tax protesters in the history of the world? He trudged from France to Philadelphia, hung around the building where they signed the Declaration of Independence, and volunteered to work for free. The Continental Congress had its doubts about saddling General George Washington with a teenage French aristocrat, but Ben Franklin wrote from Paris that the kid might be of use and, what the hell, the price was right.

So, on July 31, 1777, Congress passed a resolution appointing Lafayette a major general in the army of the United States, recognizing "his great zeal to the cause of liberty." That and the penniless rebels, in their as yet unsuccessful campaign to shake down the king of France, hoped to milk Lafayette's "illustrious family and connections" back home.

The Founding Fathers, while sticklers about taxation without representation in general, were magnanimously openminded about the French crown overtaxing French subjects to pay for the French navy to cross the Atlantic to lend a hand. *Les insurgents*, as the French referred to the Americans, wanted what all self-respecting, financially strapped terrorists want: to become state-sponsored terrorists. Without an alliance with the French government, the patriot rebels could not have won the war and President Thomas Jefferson could not have written an inaugural address warning against the evils of "entangling alliances."

The newly dubbed General Lafayette was only nineteen years old. Considering Independence Hall was also where the founders calculated that a slave equals three-fifths of a person and cooked up an electoral college that lets Florida and Ohio pick our presidents, making an adolescent who barely spoke English a major general at the age I got hired to run the cash register at a Portland pizza joint was not the worst decision ever made there.

On the one hand, the French rookie got himself shot in the calf in his very first battle. On the other hand, he was so gung ho that he cut short his recuperation and returned to duty with one leg in a boot and the other wrapped in a blanket. Which might be the first and last time in history a Frenchman shirked rest and relaxation to get back to work.

The redcoat general Lord Cornwallis sneeringly referred to Lafayette as "the boy." This put-down became all the more delightful once said boy helped cream Cornwallis at Yorktown.

In 1824, the boy came back to the United States as an old man, the Continental Army's last living general. President James Monroe invited him to return to the United States as "the nation's guest" on the eve of the golden anniversary of American independence. This seemingly simple reunion morphed into a euphoric thirteen-month victory lap in which Lafayette toured all of the then twenty-four states.

News of Lafayette's return to these shores whipped up so much collective glee that when his ship docked in New York Harbor, eighty thousand fans turned out to welcome him—in a city whose population was one hundred and twenty-three thousand. (As opposed to the measly four thousand out of a population of seven million screaming when the Beatles landed there in '64.)

On September 28, 1824, Lafayette arrived in Philadelphia to revisit the building he referred to as the Hall of Independence. Twenty thousand locals gathered there to hear what he had to say. He proclaimed, "Within these sacred walls, by a council of wise and devoted patriots, and in a style worthy of the deed itself, was boldly declared the independence of these vast United States." That event, he continued, "has begun, for the civilized world, the era of a new and of the only true social order founded on the unalienable rights of man."

That one word "only" tells the story of his life. After partaking in our revolution, Lafayette returned home and helped the French with theirs. This went well—with Jefferson's help he wrote the first draft of the Declaration of the Rights of Man and of the Citizen—until it didn't. When the Reign of Terror

LAFAYETTE

came, Lafayette, hoping to keep his head attached to his neck, made haste to the border, only to be captured by Austrians who were at war with France. So he spent five years in Austrian prisons, and not the nice ones either. Then came the restoration of the French king, the dictatorship of Napoleon, and the restoration of yet another French king. More than anyone on earth, Lafayette was mournfully aware of the uniqueness of the American republic he had fought to build.

At every stop on his itinerary Lafayette was serenaded by music composed in his honor: "Hail! Lafayette!," "Lafayette's March," "The Lafayette Waltz," "The Lafayette Rondo," "Lafayette's Welcome to North America," "Lafayette's Welcome to the United States," "Lafayette's Welcome to New York," and "Lafayette's Welcome to Philadelphia."

Cashing in on the hoopla, the souvenir trade cranked out an unprecedented pile of Lafayette-themed merch. Considering he attended a party in his honor just about every night for over a year, how many times must he have reached for a cookie and seen his own eyes staring back at him from a commemorative plate?

At the Smithsonian, I saw a lady's silk glove manufactured in honor of Lafayette's tour. His head is stamped on it right above the knuckles. Included in "Souvenir Nation," an exhibit of world historical knickknacks, the glove was displayed among glass cases containing a fence rail split by Abraham Lincoln, a "wood chip from the building in which Andrew Jackson studied law," and, my fave, Napoleon's enormous, monogrammed napkin. (What they say is true: small man, big napkin.) According to the Smithsonian's description of the Lafayette souvenir glove, when he was offered the hand of a woman wearing one at a ball in Philadelphia, he said "a few graceful words to the effect that he did not care to kiss himself."

Passing through Albany, New York, Lafayette dropped in on the widow and son of an old acquaintance, Colonel Peter Gansevoort. A descendant of Dutch pioneers who settled New York back when it was still New Netherland, Gansevoort commanded the Continental Army troops who holed up in Fort Stanwix in the Mohawk Valley, withstanding a British siege for three weeks in August 1777. The diversion of redcoat forces needed to sustain that siege contributed to the American victory at nearby Saratoga, a turning point that helped clinch the French government's decision to officially enter the war as the rebels' ally.

After he and his mother waved goodbye to Lafayette, a starstruck Peter Gansevoort Jr. wrote to his young nephews in New York City, "Posterity will be disposed to place the history of Lafayette's year in America among the legends of romance and fiction." One of those nephews would come to know a thing or two about fiction. For that boy was Herman Melville. Uncle Peter noted that Lafayette admired Gilbert Stuart's portrait of Colonel Gansevoort hanging in the house and "bore testimony to [its] accuracy." Thereafter, according to Melville biographer Hershel Parker, whenever Herman and his brother visited their grandmother's house, they made a point to park themselves in front of their grandfather's picture, partly to pay their respects to him but mostly to stand where Lafayette had stood. Parker writes, "That their own uncle and grandmother had entertained Lafayette meant that the children were in the presence, every visit, of blood kin freshly linked to the nation's earliest and most glorious epoch."

A Connecticut newspaper declared that Lafayette's pilgrimage stirred in Americans "a delirium of feeling, a tumult of the soul, from which one never wished to be awakened to the dull, sober realities of common life."

Sober reality circa 1824 included the most rancorous presidential election in American history. And that is saying something, considering that a few cases down from that Lafayette souvenir glove, the Smithsonian displayed a memento from the also iffy 2000 election: a magnifying glass used to examine Florida's hanging chads.

Though Andrew Jackson bested his three opponents, including John Quincy Adams, in the popular vote, he failed to achieve the required majority in the Electoral College, and so, per the Twelfth Amendment, the House of Representatives would choose the president the following February. In the meantime, Lafayette encountered some infuriated Jackson supporters in York, Pennsylvania, who bellowed, "If trickery and corruption make the pretentions of Adams prevail, well then, our bayonets will do justice!"

The bitter presidential campaign and the Lafayette hoopla were both amplified by the awareness of the passing of what was left of the Revolutionary generation. Lafayette's tour gave Americans one last chance to wave goodbye, not just to him, but also to the dwindling original patriots.

A crowd followed Lafayette to Quincy, Massachusetts, where he visited the ailing John Adams at his farm. "That was not the John Adams I knew," bemoaned Lafayette, though Adams reportedly said the same thing of him. After stopping at Mount Vernon, where Lafayette wept at his friend Washington's tomb, he proceeded to Charlottesville to visit the elderly Jefferson at Monticello. According to the *Charlottesville Central Gazette*, "As soon as the General drove up, Mr. Jefferson advanced to meet him, with feeble steps; but as he approached, his feelings seemed to triumph over the infirmities of age, and as the General descended they hastened into each other's arms. They embraced, again and again; tears were shed by both, and the broken expression of 'God bless you General' 'Bless you my dear Jefferson' was all that interrupted the impressive silence of the scene, except the audible sobs of many whose emotion could not be suppressed."

While Lafayette's trip stirred up citizens' tender feelings for the venerable inventors of the republic, the flip side was the countrywide angst about having to choose, for the very first time, a chief executive who was not a Founding Father. James Monroe, who had crossed the Delaware with Washington as a young lieutenant back in 1776, would be the fifth and final one.

Lafayette's secretary and traveling companion Auguste Levasseur recorded in his diary, "The nation which until the present time had been able to limit its choice to a small number of men to whom the affections of all were attached by the memories of the Revolution, found itself obliged today to start a new category due to the depletion of these men and, consequently, to open the door to the ambitions of all."

Levasseur marveled how the local papers in the towns they visited blared partisan bile about the election one day followed by sugary love letters to Lafayette the next.

Throngs of workers and tradesmen greeted Lafayette as he entered Philadelphia. Levasseur noted, "Among all these corps of artisans, one noticed especially that of the printers. Above a press, set up in the middle of the street, was this inscription: *Freedom of the press, the surest guaranty of the rights of man*. From this press poured forth abundantly odes to Lafayette and patriotic songs which they threw into our carriage as we passed by, or distributed to the people who followed."

Perusing the election coverage from town to town, Levasseur described the newspapers as "arsenals in which one finds weapons of all forms and of all characters, and they all conduct themselves at times in a very discourteous manner." Levasseur had a Frenchman's après-Terror jitters about how public displays of outrage can lead to Bastille storming and head chopping. Here in the States, he was relieved that "the exaggeration, the violence of the newspapers stays in the newspapers and never drags the masses beyond the limits of the law."

On February 9, 1825, the House elected John Quincy Adams. It was a deal that went down in history as the "corrupt bargain," even though it was a fairly by-the-book consequence of the inherently distasteful yet legal Electoral College.

Lafayette, accompanied by Levasseur, attended a party for

Adams in which Jackson showed up and clasped Adams's hands in a show of sportsmanship. "Mr. Adams appeared profoundly moved by it," wrote Levasseur, who was reassured by this gesture because it signified the stability of the republic, that the United States would outlive its fathers.

At the exact moment Lafayette's secretary decided that he could stop worrying about bayonet-toting Jacksonians storming down from Pennsylvania, he spotted a couple of them at the party: "'Well,' I said to them, 'the great question is decided, and in a manner contrary to your wishes. What are you going to do? Will you soon begin the siege of the Capital?' They began to laugh. 'You recall our threats then,' one of them said to me. 'We were, indeed, very busy shouting . . . Now that the law has spoken, we have only to obey it. We will second Adams with the same zeal as if we had supported him; but at the same time, we will hold a candle near his administration, and according to whether it will be good or bad, we will defend it or attack it."

In other words, Lafayette mania circa 1824 was specific to him and cannot be written off as the product of a simpler, more agreeable time. In the United States of America, there was no simpler, more agreeable time.

The first thing that happened when the First Continental Congress convened in Philadelphia in September of 1774 was that a delegate from Boston moved to open with a prayer. The second thing that happened, according to John Adams, was that two Episcopalians from New York and South Carolina opposed the motion "because we were so divided in religious Sentiments, some Episcopalians, some Quakers, some Anabaptists, some Presbyterians and some Congregationalists so that We could not join in the same Act of Worship."

The delegates might have spared us all centuries of friction and the body count at Gettysburg if they had just called it quits right there. But then Samuel Adams stood up. His second cousin John reported, "Mr. S. Adams arose and said he was no Bigot, and could hear a Prayer from a Gentleman of Piety and Virtue." And in a move that would have alarmed his dogmatic Quaker-hanging, Episcopalian-haranguing Puritan forebears, Sam Adams threw out the name of a local Episcopalian clergyman whose prayer the next day was a big hit among the delegates because they could all get behind his reading of the vindictive Thirty-fifth Psalm—"fight against them that fight against me."

Though, come to think of it, those fighting words might have worried the Quakers in the room—or at least some of them. Even a seemingly monotone subculture like the Religious Society of Friends was a cacophony of voices, from the neutral and nonviolent to the nonviolent yet Loyalist to the patriot "Free Quakers" and oxymoronic "Fighting Quakers" who joined the Continental Army and militias.

While it's an obvious fact that the colonials' uprising turned into a civil war between Britain and British America, in geometric terms the war cannot be drawn as two parallel lines facing each other in battle. The American side in particular was a squirming polygon of civilians, politicians, and armed forces begging to differ. And once they were done fighting the British, the Americans went back to what they were best at: infighting.

When I took a tour of Independence Hall, along with three Filipino tourists and a class of high school students from California, the most evocative object our park ranger guide pointed out to us was George Washington's original wooden armchair from the Constitutional Convention of 1787 on display in the gray-paneled Assembly Room. From that seat Washington presided over the sort of quarrels one might expect from antigovernment government representatives from rival regions of a large landmass with differing religions trying to stitch together a functioning mutual government whilst incorporating harsh checks and balances that kept it from getting too functional and thus oppressive.

Benjamin Franklin, perhaps the wisest among them, remarked, "When you assemble a number of men to have the advantage of their joint wisdom, you inevitably assemble with those men, all their prejudices, their passions, their errors of opinion, their local interests, and their selfish views."

They debated whether there should be one president or an executive committee of three, then about the length of a presidential term—four years or seven? They discussed how bad laws could be overturned, and if by presidential veto, then the king fearers had to figure out how to override said veto. They squabbled about how the lower house of the bicameral legislature should be allocated, and if by population, do slaves count? And if they count, could they count less? And if so, can we not use the actual ugly word? So how's about we refer to them as wink-wink "other persons"?

As piano player Bill Evans once described what it was like to improvise with Miles Davis, the framers muddled through "the weighty technical problem of collective coherent thinking."

In the end, thirty-nine out of fifty-five delegates agreed to sign it even though, as Franklin pointed out, expressing the misgivings of every man in the room, "there are several parts of this Constitution which I do not at present approve." However, Franklin made Washington's chair famous when he mentioned that, during the months of squabbling, he had often stared at the sun carved on the back of the chair and wondered whether it was rising or setting—which is to say, whether this was the beginning of a new republic or the end of a failed coalition. "But now," he concluded, once the document was ready to send to the states for ratification (and further disagreements), "I have the happiness to know it is a rising, and not a setting sun."

That cheerful parable turned a stick of furniture into a classic symbol of American optimism.

Bill Clinton trotted out Franklin's anecdote at the end of his final State of the Union address in 2000. "Today," he proclaimed, "because each succeeding generation of Americans has kept the fire of freedom burning brightly . . . we all still bask in the glow and the warmth of Mr. Franklin's rising sun."

Sounds good. Yet I was following in Lafayette's footsteps in the fall of 2013 in the middle of one of the most spiteful congressional budget spats of all time. A faction led by first-term Texas senator Ted Cruz, a member of the ultraconservative Tea Party wing of the Republican Party, refused to pass routine appropriations legislation to fund the federal government in the approaching fiscal year until their colleagues agreed to either delay or repeal the Patient Protection and Affordable Care Act of 2010, a law meant to make health insurance more affordable and available to more citizens (or a big government socialist conspiracy to jack up the national debt and kill small businesses and/or old people, depending on who was describing it).

Because of the lawmakers' inability to come to an agreement, the federal government was forced to shut down all nonessential government operations, including battlefields and monuments administered by the nonessential (to them but not to me) National Park Service.

It was around that time that Republican congressman Pete Sessions, another Texan, was asked about the possibility of compromising with Democrats on a budget deal that would reopen government services. Good thing Lafayette was too dead to hear his answer. "We're not French," Sessions said. "We don't surrender."

That was when I came to the conclusion that the takeaway from Benjamin Franklin's story about the carving on Washington's chair was not the forecast of a sunny future but rather Franklin's months of wondering if negotiations would collapse. That, to me, is the quintessential experience of living in the United States: constantly worrying whether or not the country is about to fall apart.

It was irritating being kept in suspense about how long the congressional tiff would keep nonessential park rangers from helping me do my even less essential job. I cannot imagine how a Lakota domestic violence victim—turned away from the shuttered women's shelter on her reservation because its federal funding ran out—would interpret the wood carving on Washington's chair, but I'm guessing she would have more pressing concerns.

I wish that the founders had had the foresight to hang on to and enshrine another one of Independence Hall's chairs, the one that Benjamin Rush mentioned in a letter to John Adams about how Thomas Jefferson objected when his colleagues in the Continental Congress considered organizing a fast day, which Jefferson pooh-poohed as too religious. Rush reminded Adams, "You rose and defended the motion, and in reply to Mr. Jefferson's objections to Christianity you said you were sorry to hear such sentiments from a gentleman whom you so highly respected and with whom you agreed upon so many subjects, and that it was the only instance you had ever known of a man of sound sense and real genius that was an enemy to Christianity. You suspected, you told me, that you had offended him, but that he soon convinced you to the contrary by crossing the room and taking a seat in the chair next to you."

Who knows what happened to that particular chair. It could have burned during the British occupation of Philadelphia in the winter of 1777–78, when firewood was scarce. But it might have been a more helpful, sobering symbolic object than that chair with the rising sun. Then perhaps citizens making pilgrimages to Independence Hall could file past the chair Jefferson walked across an aisle to sit in, and we could all ponder the amount of respect, affection, and wishy-washy give-and-take needed to keep a house divided in reasonable repair.

Months before the shutdown, I had purchased nonrefundable plane tickets to Virginia so my twin sister, Amy, and I could take her thirteen-year-old son, Owen, to Colonial Williamsburg, Jefferson's Monticello, and Yorktown, where we planned to ponder the revolution's high-water mark of Franco-American cooperation. Once we got down there, the shutdown was in full swing. I fretted over whether Congress would engage in enough American-American cooperation to let the National Park Service reopen Yorktown Battlefield in time for Yorktown Day, the anniversary of the British surrender to the Americans and the French.

At Montpelier, the (privately run and therefore open) Virginia home of the Constitution's architect, James Madison, I nervously clicked on the news on my phone every few minutes, hoping for a deal that would reopen Colonial National Historical Park. Filing past the cardboard cutout of Lafayette seated in the mansion's fancy dining room, I couldn't help wondering if the separation of powers inscribed in Madison's brainchild were meant to arouse quite so much separation.

To my relief, the shutdown finally ended a couple of days before the Yorktown Day commemorations commenced. And at the Franco-American hootenanny put on by the town, it was downright poignant when the French visitors who were there to remember the French blood spilled in Virginia fields and Chesapeake waters sang their own super-violent national anthem composed during their own gory revolution.

"They should have sung that angry-men song from *Les Miz*," said the nephew, a thespian who was missing rehearsals for his teen theater company's production of *Singin' in the Rain* to join me in Virginia.

"Actually, that song is set during the Paris Uprising of 1832," I told him.

"'Actually, that song is set during the Paris Uprising of 1832,'" he repeated back to me in a snotty egghead voice.

I can't really blame the kid for confusing a later French rebellion with the official French Revolution of 1789, because France had so many brutal hiccups after that, yo-yoing from republic back to monarchy to the so-called republics of Napoleon and his heirs with the odd riotous bloodbath in between. Which is why the French citizens who showed up at the Yorktown festivities and sang "La Marseillaise" refer to their current government as the Fifth Republic.

Revolutionary France was no place for a moderate like Lafayette, whose rough draft of the Declaration of the Rights of Man and of the Citizen was written as a preamble for a new constitution in the constitutional monarchy he hoped to establish, with the king as a figurehead—with a head. But when he proclaimed to the French people, "All men are created free and equal" with "certain unalienable rights," including "the right to hold and express opinions," every commoner and guttersnipe believed him. And so instead of spending the early days of the revolution luxuriating in high-minded Independence Hall–style constitutional debates, Lafayette had to keep riding his horse around Paris, frantically trying to talk ferocious crowds out of hanging priests and other grandees. "I have already saved the lives of six people about to be hanged in different sections of the city," he wrote in July of 1789. "The people are insane, drunk with power; they will not listen to me forever . . . The minute I am gone, they lose their minds."

Because Lafayette's American Revolution bona fides gave him credibility with the people, he was named commander of the National Guard, the de facto top cop of France. After the storming of the Bastille, he ordered the symbol of the old regime to be torn down. (He sent George Washington the big Bastille key that still hangs in Mount Vernon's hall.)

That October, when mothers fed up with bread shortages led thousands of Parisians on a thirteen-mile hike to Versailles to confront King Louis XVI, Lafayette escorted them, hoping to keep tempers in check. He couldn't stop them from breaking into the palace and murdering a couple of guards whose heads they jabbed onto pikes, but he did save the lives of the king and queen, for the moment, by trotting Marie Antoinette out onto a balcony and kissing her hand, thereby pacifying the mob into letting the royal family come back to Paris with them in a carriage instead of in a hearse. Eventually the revolution's radicals turned on Lafayette, who had to flee France to avoid the king and queen's fate on the "National Razor," the guillotine.

When Count Rochambeau, the general who had commanded the French forces backing up Washington's Continental Army at Yorktown, was locked up by the radicals for "treason" in the Conciergerie, the same prison that housed Marie Antoinette, he lectured his jailors, "I cannot believe in this era of equality a former aristocrat has no rights except to march to the scaffold before anybody else, and to be the last man to prove his innocence. Those are not the principles I learned from Washington, my colleague and my friend, when we were fighting side by side for American independence."

Researching Lafayette's role in the Women's March of 1789 required me to revisit my least favorite building on earth, the morally and architecturally bankrupt compendium of gilded nonsense and silken flimflam known as the Château de Versailles. So afterward I rewarded myself with a stop at the nearby Villa Savoye, a modernist country house of the early 1930s designed by architect cousins Le Corbusier and Pierre Jeanneret. The stark concrete edifice plopped into a field surrounded by woods is much more in keeping with my uptight Protestant aesthetic. Then it hit me how the streamlined architectural ideas that made that house a blank, low-key bunker from which to look outside and succumb to the trees' embrace would be dumbed down through the decades into the national retail chains' crass, cheapo big-box stores now besmirching the Montana valley I grew up in.

In other words, ideas, when implemented, turn into precedents with unpredictable and potentially disturbing consequences. As the British historian and politician Lord Acton described the effect that our Revolutionary War had on our French allies, "What the French took from the Americans was their theory of revolution, not their theory of government—their cutting, not their sewing."

A couple of days after Yorktown Day, the subject of the decades of instability unleashed by the French Revolution, as opposed to the governmental continuity spawned by the American Revolution, came up when I was visiting Monticello. I was talking to the British-born historian Andrew Jackson O'Shaughnessy, director of the Robert H. Smith International Center for Jefferson Studies, in his office down the hill from Jefferson's house. O'Shaughnessy is the author of *The Men Who Lost America*, a graceful, perceptive portrait of Great Britain's politicians and commanders of the Revolutionary War. He told me, "It was Hannah Arendt who really made that point well. What she wanted to do was understand revolutions—why so many fail. And why the American Revolution seems almost a model for a successful one because they already had experience in self-government."

He was referring to the German-born theorist's 1963 book, *On Revolution*. In it, Arendt asserts that the French revolutionaries, as the subjects of an absolute monarch (not a constitutional monarch, as in Great Britain), "had no experiences to fall back upon, only ideas and principles untested by reality." Thus the French Revolution, she alleges, turned into "an intoxication whose chief element was the crowd." Which was a fine legacy for igniting later flare-ups, like the one that made good fodder for the Victor Hugo novel tarted up into a musical. But for anchoring a reasonably just government capable of handling the peaceful transfer of power for decades to come? Not so much.

Arendt suggests that the American colonists revolted "not because of any specifically revolutionary or rebellious spirit but because the inhabitants of the colonies" benefited from—and here she cites John Adams—"'the right to assemble . . . in their town halls, there to deliberate upon the public affairs.'" The colonists, Arendt continues, "went to the town assemblies, as their representatives later were to go to the famous Conventions, neither exclusively because of duty nor, and even less, to serve their own interests but most of all because they enjoyed the discussions, the deliberations, and the making of decisions."

The context of Patrick Henry's explosive slogan "Give me liberty or give me death!" backs up Arendt's assertion. Henry was speaking in 1775 at a meeting organized by thwarted members of Virginia's House of Burgesses after the colony's royal governor dissolved the House for the first time since it had convened at Jamestown way back in 1619. And why did the crown's man in Virginia pull the plug on the oldest legislative assembly of elected representatives in British America? Because the burgesses had organized a day of "fasting, Humiliation and prayer" to show Bostonians moral support in light of the so-called Intolerable Acts that Parliament had passed as punishment for what was then referred to as the Destruction of the Tea, including closing the city's port.

According to a version of Henry's speech cobbled together later by his biographer William Wirt, Henry declared, "The question before the House is one of awful moment to this country." His rhetoric heats up from there, culminating in the sizzling slogan we all know. But he wasn't some crank on a street corner. He was addressing his fellow representatives just as Virginia subjects of the crown had been doing for a century and a half.

Moreover, if Arendt is right, Henry *enjoyed* it. How else to explain showbiz wordplay like "Our chains are forged! Their clanking may be heard on the plains of Boston!"

To Arendt's point about post-revolution stability deriving from pre-revolutionary experience in self government, it's worth remembering that two of Henry's less chatty fellow burgesses became the first and third presidents of the United States.

Andrew O'Shaughnessy, referring to the masterminds of the 2013 government shutdown and no doubt alluding to the freshman senator who was its ringleader, told me, "Experience is terribly important. You'll notice that the congressmen who want to hold up the government are all junior people and new to the game. And of course they will say, 'Oh, it's Washington cynicism, where they all compromise and work out backroom deals.' But that's actually how democracy works."

Which is exactly how government operations resumed on October 17, 2013: a bipartisan group of old-school senators with the combined age of Stonehenge started hashing out a bargain drafted by third-term moderate Republican Susan Collins of Maine, who, prior to her election sixteen years earlier, had spent twelve years working behind the scenes as a legislative aide to her predecessor.

During the shutdown hubbub, I happened to read the message Franklin Roosevelt delivered to Congress in 1934 on the one hundredth anniversary of Lafayette's death. "A century ago," he said, "President Andrew Jackson, in communicating the melancholy news of the death of Lafayette to the Congress of the United States, called it 'afflicting intelligence.'" Mentioning Jackson's orders to the army and navy to pay tribute to

Lafayette as "'the distinguished friend of the United States,'" Roosevelt noted, "Congress, with rare felicity, added to this phrase, 'the friend of Washington, and the friend of liberty.'"

I cannot think of a more euphemistic, upper-crust, dry martini of a zinger than "rare felicity," FDR's wry acknowledgment that every now and then, even a bunch of backbiting blowhards like the United States Congress can temporarily come together with their president to mourn the death of one of the few people, places, or things they and their fidgety constituents have ever agreed on. As a Frenchman who represented neither North nor South, East nor West, left nor right, Yankees nor Red Sox, Lafayette has always belonged to all of us.

In 1777, after young Lafayette had been in the Continental Army for about five months, he wrote to George Washington from across the camp at Valley Forge: "When I was in Europe I thought that here almost every man was a lover of liberty . . . You can conceive my astonishment when I saw that toryism"— loyalty to the British crown—"was as openly professed as whiggism," the republican creed of the patriots. Back in France, he recalled, "I believed that all good Americans were united together." But that was before he got here. In his reply, Washington acknowledged his fellow Americans' "fatal tendency of disunion."

The purpose of Lafayette's letter was to buck up his friend and mentor in light of a plot orchestrated by a few Continental Army officers and congressmen to oust Washington as commander. Lafayette, who may have been more appalled by this conspiracy than Washington himself, worried that the patriots' greatest enemy might not be Great Britain's formidable military. "I see plainly that America can defend herself if proper measures are taken," he wrote, adding ominously, "and now I begin to fear she should be lost by herself and her own sons."

The congressmen and officers who horrified Lafayette by plotting behind Washington's back probably could have spared a moment to toast Washington for the miracle of keeping his underfunded hodgepodge of newbies from disintegrating. Especially since they were confronting such a venerable, well-oiled fighting force led by seasoned commanders who came from the sort of military families that had for generations made sure that there would always be an England. But Washington's critics were way too preoccupied with how he had just hemorrhaged twenty percent of his troops by losing two major battles, thereby handing the British control of the capital, Philadelphia—all within three weeks. So while Lafayette's faith in his comrade turned out to be well founded in the long run, Washington's frenemies cannot be written off as mere petty schemers indulging in what one of his supporters belittled as "the shafts of envy and malevolence."

Oh, the men in the Second Continental Congress were not lacking envy and malevolence any more than the sweethearts of the 113th Congress. Yet one of the naysayers wrote to John Adams about Washington's recent failures, despairing of what would happen "if our congress can witness these things with composure and suffer them to pass without an enquiry." In other words, technically, the congressional job description at that moment required kicking George Washington when he was down. The polite name for it is civilian oversight.

The thing that drew me to Lafayette as a subject—that he was that rare object of agreement in the ironically named United States—kept me coming back to why that made him unique. Namely, that we the people have never agreed on much of anything. Other than a bipartisan consensus on barbecue and Meryl Streep, plus that time in 1942 when everyone from Bing Crosby to Oregonian schoolchildren heeded FDR's call to scrounge up rubber for the war effort, disunity is the through line in the national plot—not necessarily as a failing, but as a free people's privilege. And thanks to Lafayette and his cohorts in Washington's army, plus the king of France and his navy, not to mention the founding dreamers who clearly did not think through what happens every time one citizen's pursuit of happiness infuriates his neighbors, getting on each other's nerves is our *right*.

In 1777, the nineteen-year-old Lafayette lit out for the New World for a few reasons, including a juvenile lust for glory, the appeal of escaping his nagging in-laws, boredom with the court shenanigans of Versailles, and a head full of Enlightenment chitchat about liberty and equality. But the boy's most obvious motivation in crossing the Atlantic to join the American colonists' war against the British crown was probably the simple glaring fact that before his second birthday, a British cannonball killed his soldier father in the Seven Years' War.

The Battle of Minden, in which Lafayette's father died (and

a young Cornwallis fought), was just one of the many British triumphs of 1759, the so-called annus mirabilis in which they trounced the French from Quebec to India to the extent that one member of Parliament snorted, "Our bells are worn threadbare with ringing for victories." Per the humiliating peace treaty that ended the war in 1763, France had to give almost all of French Canada to Britain, as well as Louisiana to Spain to make up for the Spanish loss of Florida. Thus the massive chunk of North America claimed by France for more than two centuries—from the Atlantic to the Great Lakes to the Gulf of Mexico—was downsized to scraps. They were left with fishing rights off Newfoundland and a couple of foggy islands where they were allowed to dry cod and presumably their tears.

Thus Lafayette's private contempt for Englishmen mirrored the larger French national hatred of Great Britain—a grudge the American rebels later exploited to drum up French support.

The death of his father at the hands of British forces merely provided the boy with a specific target at a young age. Soldiering in general was his destiny, just as it had been for his father before him and most of the grandfathers before that, stretching back to Joan of Arc and the Crusades.

War being the family business explains the boy's ample birth name: Marie-Joseph-Paul-Yves-Roch-Gilbert du Motier, future Marquis de Lafayette. "I was baptized like a Spaniard," he joked in his memoirs, "with the name of every conceivable saint who might offer me more protection in battle."

It might be more specific to say that dying young in combat was the family business. All those chivalrous young casualties felled far from home may even explain how the family Lafayette sustained such a long line of warriors for hundreds of years: few of them had to grow up around jangled relatives damaged by war. In my family, one shell-shocked World War II vet flinching at firecrackers every Fourth of July for fifty years personified the painful side effects of military service. Even years after my uncle's death, Independence Day is not only the anniversary of Jefferson's Declaration. To me, it's the anniversary of July 4, 1946, when fireworks hurled Uncle John A., who had just gotten home from the Philippines, into a combat flashback so real and frightening that he pushed his poor date down into what he thought was a foxhole and slammed a park bench right on top of her.

According to Lafayette's assessment of his warmongering ancestors, "so large a proportion of fathers and sons were killed on the field of battle that the family's misfortunes in war became a kind of proverb throughout the province."

Then, as now, the province in question, Auvergne, was one of the least-populated regions in Europe, a mostly rural slice of central France known for agricultural products like blue cheese made from the milk of the many cows grazing its green, volcanic hills. Gilbert, as the redheaded boy was called, was born in 1757 in the Château de Chavaniac, his paternal manor house in a tiny hamlet around three hundred miles south of Paris. And by tiny, I mean Chavaniac's population in 2007 was 291.

Curious what present-day Parisians think of the people of Auvergne, I asked a friend who lives there to ask around. And with the traditional Parisian generosity of spirit, a woman named

Agnes reported back, "They are especially known for being miserly." She added that the ones who move from Auvergne to Paris tend to become café waiters and are therefore of "the lower class." This was an amusing if mean revelation, because, to American tourists, Paris café waiters are the front line of making us feel like rubes. The uppity servers rolling their eyes at our poorly pronounced drink orders are actually former farm kids? It reminds me of how the raggedy Continental Army regulars mistook French enlisted men for officers because their flashy uniforms were festooned with pink collars and red velvet lapels. Agnes did caution against lumping Lafayette with the hayseeds who were his boyhood playmates, adding, "Lafayette was a nobleman and therefore not in the same category as the men I just described."

Lafayette might have been a nobleman, but he was still a country boy. According to his memoirs, the highlight of his childhood was when the region was terrorized by some sort of hybrid wolf-hyena-dog monster—the exact species remains up for debate to this day. Whatever it was, the Beast of Gévaudan, as it was known, stalked the countryside mauling peasants. The eight-year-old Lafayette, with "an enthusiasm for glorious deeds," went on the hunt. The fact that a child that age was allowed to go out looking for the four-legged serial killer that the king had dispatched his personal gun-bearer to track down speaks of an older, hands-off parenting style. "Meeting it was the object of all my walks," Lafayette remembered, foreshadowing his later can-do courage on the battlefield.

The Château de Chavaniac looms at the top of a small hill,

a dark gray rectangle bookended by a pair of round feudal towers. Surfaced in natural rocks instead of cut stone, it has a rough texture that makes it appear even older than its medieval roots. Visiting the place today provides insight into Lafayette's later soft spot for the American bumpkins he served with—as well as an understanding of just how imprecise the French word "château" is. The rustic gloom of the Château de Chavaniac is a Woody Guthrie song compared to the Liberace concert that is the Château de Versailles.

I arrive too early on an icy December morning for the château to be open and decide to kill some time over a cup of tea in the village *bar-tabac*. The waitress and a pair of patrons seem surprised to see an outsider pop in, but they welcome me, along with my driver, an overdressed city slicker from Lyon. Given the proximity of Lafayette's house, the townsfolk must be used to the occasional American looky-loo passing through town. Still, the place feels like enough of an old-fangled French time warp that when an elderly local comes in from the cold, the driver sizes up the new arrival and whispers with absolute certainty, "He's here for his 9:30 white wine." Sure enough, a glass of the stuff is placed before him on the bar. I must have some puritanical look on my face, because the driver laughs and says, "Welcome to France."

The Château de Chavaniac is a museum open to the public, but only in warmer months, because the old rock pile lacks heat. Xavier Comte, a kindly official with the regional tourism bureau, has agreed to open the house for my benefit, possibly for the simple reason that Lafayette would want him to.

Monsieur Comte is game to show me around Chavaniac as long as I promise to dress warmly because of the area's "rigorous winters." The temperature the day of my visit is around twenty-five degrees Fahrenheit, which is barely noticeable in the dry mountains where I grew up. Yet damp European winters always bite harder, as if every day below freezing carries within it bitter memories of all the other cold days since Hannibal crossed the Alps.

My e-mails to Monsieur Comte before my arrival benefited from the polish of Google Translate, so my laughable French takes him by surprise. I had one of those impractical educations in the language. I learned to fake my way through Proust, but a quarter century later, all that's left is me slaughtering addresses in taxis.

As a kindness, Monsieur Comte starts speaking French wonderfully, hilariously slowly, as though I were a brain-damaged simpleton who had imbibed too much of the 9:30 wine. We move from the original, medieval areas of the house to rooms added later and adorned with Louis-something-style chairs or, in the chamber where Lafayette was born, toile wallpaper. Comte mentions (I'm pretty sure) Lafayette's warrior ancestors and the beloved grandmother who raised him here after his mother, distraught over her husband's death, returned to Paris to stay with her family.

At the age of eleven, Lafayette's mother wrenched him away from his grandmother's pastoral home, summoning him to Paris and school. "I felt not a bit of curiosity to see the capital," he complained. His mother's family was even fancier than his father's. Nobility originally from Brittany, they descended from King Louis IX and were well connected to the court of Louis XV.

At twelve, the boy without a father was left motherless as well. He was suddenly the richest orphan in France after his mother and her grandfather died within days of each other, adding vast lands in Brittany to Lafayette's paternal holdings in Auvergne. So he was loaded if bereft, pointing out, "I had not thought but to lament my mother, never having experienced any need for money."

Besides the money and land, Lafayette inherited a six-foot-tall hole in his heart that only a father figure like George Washington could fill. According to Jefferson, Lafayette's "foible is a canine appetite for popularity." The orphaned only child's puppyish yearning for kinship is at the root of his accomplishments in America, the source of his keyed-up eagerness to distinguish himself, particularly on the battlefield. He tended to confuse glory with love.

After his mother's death, young Lafayette, "burning with desire to be in uniform," was sent to Versailles to follow in his great-grandfather's footsteps and join the Black Musketeers, the aristocratic horsey set serving as the king's household troops. He also attended the riding school at Versailles along with three future kings of France. What with his haughty blood, the rarefied company he kept, and, not least, his considerable wealth, this eligible bachelor was off the market before he turned fifteen.

The powerful duc d'Ayen, Jean de Noailles, the brigadier

general of the king's armies, arranged a marriage between Lafayette and his daughter Adrienne, age twelve. But when the
duke's wife found out, she was appalled at the idea of making a
child bride out of her child and raised a ruckus. The duchess
agreed to the arrangement only on the condition that the children wait a couple of years—and that Adrienne be kept in the
dark. Even after the wedding in 1774, Adrienne's mother vetoed
consummation, sequestering the two in separate bedrooms.

The Lafayette-Noailles wedding reception was a big-enough
deal that King Louis XV attended. I hope he was hungry, if the
menu for the soirée that's on display at the Château de Chavaniac is to be believed: there were thirty salads alone, plus roasted
meats of just about every bird and mammal in France, with the
possible exception of barbecued Beast of Gévaudan.

Louis XV died a few weeks after the Lafayette nuptials
(from smallpox, not the opulent wedding spread), and his
nineteen-year-old grandson was crowned Louis XVI in 1774.
Rich blue bloods such as Lafayette and his recent bride were,
theoretically, ideal additions to the new Austrian-born queen's
guest list. That is until Marie Antoinette literally laughed Lafayette off her dance floor. "The favor I enjoyed among the
young nobility was short-lived," Lafayette admitted. As his
friend the Comte de Ségur put it, the yokel from Auvergne
"seemed awkward, danced badly and spoke little." Witnessing
Lafayette blatantly botch a dance with Marie Antoinette at one
of her swanky balls, Ségur winced that Lafayette "proved so
clumsy and so awkward that the queen laughed at him." According to Lafayette, "My awkward country manners—and a

certain self-respect—made it impossible for me to adapt entirely to the required graces of the court."

However, he was smooth enough to get past his mother-in-law's obstacles keeping him from his wife's boudoir. Adrienne was soon pregnant with their first child. His father-in-law was just as controlling, setting up Lafayette with a dull if distinguished job as a court flunky to the king's brother and heir, the Count of Provence. Part of Lafayette's marriage arrangement included a commission as an officer in the prestigious family cavalry unit, the Noailles Regiment, and he wanted to stay there and pursue a military career like his forefathers. Lafayette must have suspected that the only thing the portly Provence was likely to attack was a lunch buffet. And so he insulted his prospective employer, thereby talking his way out of the job, much to his father-in-law's dismay. Said Lafayette, "I did not hesitate to be disagreeable to preserve my independence." Spoken like every only child ever.

Lafayette happily continued soldiering, and three noteworthy things happened: news of the first shots in the American Revolution reached France; the Comte de Broglie, commander of the Army of the East and thus the general Lafayette was serving under at a training camp in the city of Metz, invited him to become a member of his military Masonic lodge; and Lafayette joined his brother Masons at dinner in Metz with the Duke of Gloucester, who made a big impression on Lafayette by letting rip a biting condemnation of his own brother's treatment of his American subjects—his brother being Britain's King George III.

After that, Lafayette swooned in his memoirs, "I gave my heart to the Americans."

Incidentally, a rather action-packed equestrian statue commemorates Lafayette's political arousal in Metz. He has his sword drawn with one hand while the other reins in his twisting horse, as if he has suddenly decided to ride through the night to Boston Harbor. The American Knights of Columbus donated the bronze sculpture to the city in 1920 both as a nod to the French contributions to the founding of the United States and as a grief-stricken token of remembrance for the American and French casualties of World War I. The Nazis tore down the statue out of spite when they occupied the city in World War II. In 2004, Lafayette and his horse were restored to their rightful spot before the Governor's Palace on the sixtieth anniversary of the liberation of Metz in 1944, when the U.S. Third Army under General George S. Patton defeated the Wehrmacht forces controlling the town.

As for Lafayette becoming a Freemason: one did not have to be an orphaned only child to be predisposed to joining a mysterious brotherhood with snazzy secret handshakes, but it didn't hurt. Famous Freemason Benjamin Franklin said of the group, "While each lodge is created from individual members and while individuality is treasured, lodges are designed to be sociable and to encourage mutual works." What a perfect arrangement for Lafayette, who harbored contradictory ambitions to both fit in *and* stick out.

Lafayette may have been in a Masonic lodge when he first heard the names of his fellow Masons Franklin and George

Washington and their struggle against their government. (Fun fact: Washington went on to lay the cornerstone of the U.S. Capitol building in 1793 wearing a Masonic apron embroidered for him by Adrienne, Lafayette's wife.)

Devoted to principles of liberty, equality, and religious tolerance—which, dear Internet, is not necessarily the same thing as Satanism—Masonic lodges became the de facto clubhouses of the Age of Reason, attracting the French Enlightenment writers Voltaire, Denis Diderot, and Jean-Jacques Rousseau, whose influential book *The Social Contract* famously despaired, "Man is born free; and everywhere he is in chains."

Hanging around Masonic lodges back in Paris, Lafayette came under the sway of Abbé Guillaume Raynal, a defrocked Jesuit priest turned writer. When Lafayette met him in 1775, the first volume of Raynal's 1770 *History of the Two Indies* had already been banned, which is to say it was a popular success, the Catholic Church's Index of Forbidden Books being the unofficial bestseller list of the day. Chronicling centuries of subjugation of the peoples of Asia, Africa, and the Americas, Raynal took the European monarchies to task for colonialism and slavery. (An especially inconvenient opinion in France, an empire financially and chemically dependent on the sugar cultivated by slaves in its Caribbean colonies.) Raynal's abolitionist beliefs had a profound effect on Lafayette, who went on to join the French abolitionist group the Society of the Friends of the Blacks and to purchase a cinnamon plantation in French Guiana to emancipate its slaves, educate them, and pay them for their labor.

At the advent of the American Revolution, Raynal's proclamation that it is "an inalienable and natural right" for oppressed peoples to rise up against their overlords especially struck a chord with Lafayette. Raynal practically dared colonists to revolt, taunting, "Do not bother us with your complaints and learn to accept your unhappiness if you are unwilling to become free."

Lafayette's friend and fellow soldier Ségur accompanied him to various meals and diatribes with Raynal. Echoing Raynal's equating freedom with bravery, Ségur wrote, "Liberty, whatever its language, appealed to us by its courage."

Increasingly obsessed with the American rebels, Lafayette conceded that he "thought of nothing else but raising my banner and adding my colors to theirs." Of course, an added incentive was that France was uncharacteristically and annoyingly at peace. Lafayette, a self-described "ardent lover of laurels," was well aware that he wasn't going to win battlefield glory without any actual battles.

Such was his craving for armed conflict that the birth of his daughter Henriette in December 1775 barely registered.

While history might be full of exemplary fathers, recorded history is not where to find them. As Lafayette was trying to figure out how to go about ditching his family to head for the colonies and fame, a colonist who would help him do so was en route to Paris, unbeknownst to his own wife and son.

In March of 1776, Silas Deane, a delegate to the Continental Congress from Connecticut, wrote a letter from Philadelphia to his wife, Elizabeth, informing her that he would not be coming home. He asked her to keep taking care of the twelve-year-old stepson he stuck her with months ago, the offspring of Deane's previous dead wife. Deane implored Elizabeth to "guard his youth from anything dangerous or dishonorable." Surely a simple task, safety and decorum being the top priorities of the hormonal preteen male. "I can but feel for the pain I must give you by this adventure," he whimpered, adding, "I wish as much as any man for the enjoyment of domestic ease." One wonders how the words "domestic ease" came across to the beleaguered babysitter of a dead woman's spawn. "I am about to enter on the great stage of Europe," he boasted to the woman saddled with a boy about to enter the not-so-great stage of puberty.

I've encountered my fair share of war reenactors over the years, but I've never seen a reenactment of this banal predicament: a tired woman in a dark house answering a child who is supposed to be asleep that she has no idea when Daddy's coming home. Elizabeth never saw her husband again, since she died while he was abroad—the wives of Silas Deane apparently enjoying the life expectancy of the male Lafayettes.

In its mission letter to Deane on March 3, 1776, the congressional Committee of Secret Correspondence correctly predicted, "There is a great appearance we shall come to a total separation from Great Britain." Which is why Deane was to make haste to France. For France, said the missive signed by, among others, Ben Franklin and John Jay, "would be looked upon as the power, whose friendship it would be fittest for us to obtain and cultivate."

Deane was charged with convincing the French foreign minister, the Comte de Vergennes, that a defeat for Britain would be a political and fiscal win for France. He was to hit up the minister for "clothing and arms for twenty five thousand men with a suitable quantity of ammunition, and one hundred field pieces."

Deane was to pretend to be a merchant (which was in fact his profession) in Paris accumulating goods to trade with Indians as well as a tourist eager to see "so famous a city."

The assignment demanded a certain finesse, and not just because, like most endeavors of the Continental Congress, it was an act of treason. France, still licking its wounds from the Seven Years' War, was wary about antagonizing Great Britain. The court of Louis XVI could not afford to pay for another full-blown war so soon after the last expensive drubbing.

(By the way, neither could Great Britain, which was one reason it lost. The tax laws that triggered the colonial rebellion in the first place were meant to replenish Britain's empty coffers after the Seven Years' War. Or as it's called in the United States, the French and Indian War. One of Parliament's motivations was to make the colonists chip in on paying for their own defense.)

Besides being broke, the French did not want to risk agitating the "roast beefs," as they called the British, when the American rebels were so clearly outmanned and outgunned.

And yet. While French financial resources were finite, France's contempt for Great Britain was not. The national grudge was a bottomless, interminable, renewable resource of hate. As George Washington put it in his presidential fare-well address of 1796, that kind of bad blood is a form of slavery. And George Washington knew from slavery. "The nation which indulges towards another a habitual hatred or a habitual fond-ness is in some degree a slave," he wrote. "It is a slave to its ani-mosity or to its affection, either of which is sufficient to lead it astray from its duty and its interest."

Luckily for Washington, the French foreign minister Ver-gennes had already been conniving to secretly fund the Ameri-cans as a bargain-basement method of harassing the British when Silas Deane showed up at his door.

The shadowy figure who had been plotting behind the scenes with Vergennes was, of all people, France's greatest living dramatist, Pierre-Augustin Caron de Beaumarchais, author of the hit play *The Barber of Seville*. This came about, oh, the usual way, when the foreign minister enlisted the playwright to go to London and apprehend a vexing cross-dressing ex-spy. Vergennes was so impressed by the mind of Figaro, *The Barber of Seville*'s shrewd protagonist, that he figured Beaumarchais would have the wiles to ensnare such slippery prey. That and the author's celebrity were sure to open doors.

The object of Beaumarchais's hunt, the Chevalier d'Éon de Beaumont, had previously served France as both a male soldier in the Seven Years' War and a female secret agent who infil-trated the Russian monarchy, successfully befriending and con-vincing a Russian czarina not to become an ally of France's enemy Great Britain. No one was entirely sure of his/her gen-der, and he/she kept them guessing. D'Éon had been extorting the government of Louis XV from his London home for years, threatening to turn over to the British some old French secret plans from the Seven Years' War to invade England. After the death of Louis, the government wanted d'Éon and the documents returned home to France.

Beaumarchais easily scored an invite to a dinner party among the smart set that d'Éon was to attend. Confronting him—for he was dressed as a man at the time—Beaumarchais tried to convince d'Éon to return to France to sort out his problems with the regime. D'Éon said he would, but he was afraid of being locked up in the Bastille, especially since he revealed to Beaumarchais that he was a woman. Whether or not that was true—and technically it wasn't, based on a postmortem examination of d'Éon's anatomically male corpse years later—the professionally imaginative Beaumarchais concocted a theatrical solution. After handing over the invasion plans, d'Éon would be welcomed back to France and receive his military pension as long as he agreed to live out the rest of his life as a woman. Which happened!

Meanwhile, the host of the dinner party where Beaumarchais met d'Éon was none other than the man George III denounced as "that devil Wilkes." John Wilkes, the rabble-rousing journalist, lord mayor of London, and pen pal of the Boston Sons of Liberty, was one of the most vocal members of Parliament who opposed the conflict in America. He denounced it as "an unjust, ruinous, murderous and felonious war," predicting, "The whole continent will be dismembered from Great Britain, and the wide arch of the raised empire fall."

At Wilkes's house, Beaumarchais ended up befriending the Virginian Arthur Lee, then officially representing the colonies of Massachusetts and New Jersey in England whilst unofficially acting as an informant to the Continental Congress's Secret Committee of Correspondence. Lee jumped at the chance to buttonhole a prominent Frenchman, making a case for American independence as well as an appeal for aid. Lee also dangled the prospect of future riches, predicting a lucrative postwar commercial relationship with whichever nation helped the colonies become a country. Lee told him, "We offer France, as a reward for its secret aid, a secret treaty of commerce," pledging "all the advantages of that commerce which for a century America has enriched England."

Beaumarchais was hooked. He wrote to Vergennes, "The Americans will triumph but they must be assisted in their struggle, for if they lose, they will turn against us for not having helped them. We are not yet ready for war ourselves, but we must prepare and, while doing so, we must send secret aid to the Americans in the most prudent way."

Running guns to the rebels would not only undermine Britain's military and economic stability, it could also lead to a future windfall for France—and, Beaumarchais realized, the gunrunner. He penned a letter to Louis XVI imploring the king to secretly help the Americans, adding, "If your majesty does not have a more clever man at hand" to handle the logistics, then he would volunteer for the job. By that age, the playwright had already been a watchmaker, a failed businessman, and the harp teacher to the daughters of Louis XV, so he was game for moonlighting as a covert arms dealer, in between writing *The Marriage of Figaro* and publishing the complete works of Voltaire.

Vergennes was intrigued but not convinced, rebuffing Arthur Lee at Versailles and declining, for the moment, to pass along Beaumarchais's gushy letter to the king. In order to make an informed decision, the foreign minister dispatched a clandestine fact-finder to Philadelphia, a former soldier who had been to America before, Achard de Bonvouloir. Bonvouloir was to assess the rebels' chances at defeating Britain, and he was also asked to determine the Americans' dedication to the rebellion, which was still uncertain in the summer of 1775.

Though the first shots of the Revolution had been fired in Lexington and Concord on April 19, followed by the Battle of Bunker Hill in June, it was nevertheless wise to question whether Americans were committed for the long haul to a war against their mother country. For one thing, there was a suspicious hopefulness in the way colonists still referred to the offending redcoats of the aforementioned dustups in Massachusetts as "Parliament Troops" or the "Ministerial Army," which is to say the hired guns of Parliament and the prime minister, not the still-beloved George III.

On July 8, three weeks after Bunker Hill, Congress adopted the so-called Olive Branch Petition, a declaration of loyalty to George III from "your still faithful colonists" and "your American people." Mostly written by the pacifist Pennsylvanian John Dickinson (to the objection of John Adams and the Massachusetts delegation), the petition beseeched His Majesty to stop the war by taking the colonies' side against Parliament. In other words, the most ardent republicans since the fall of Rome were asking their king to help them prevail over the representative legislature of the world's oldest constitutional monarchy, the great symbol and protector of British freedom.

From the Stamp Act of 1765 and the Townshend Revenue Act of 1767 to the Tea Act of 1773 and the Coercive, aka "Intolerable," Acts of 1774 (conceived as punishment for the Boston Tea Party), it was increasingly vindictive parliamentary legislation that turned lawyers into traitors and farmers into insurgents. As Thomas Jefferson wrote in *A Summary View of the Rights of British America* in 1774, "Scarcely have our minds been able to emerge from the astonishment into which one stroke of parliamentary thunder has involved us, before another more heavy, and more alarming, is fallen on us."

In fact, way back at the beginning of the crisis in 1766, Benjamin Franklin gave testimony before Parliament regarding the furor in the colonies over the Stamp Act. When asked what Americans thought of Parliament before the act, Franklin replied, "They considered the parliament as the great bulwark and security of their liberties and privileges, and always spoke of it with the utmost respect and veneration." To the follow-up question—"And have they not still the same respect for Parliament?"—Franklin revealed, "No; it is greatly lessened."

The Olive Branch Petition came up during my chat with historian Andrew O'Shaughnessy at Monticello. I confessed that, as an American, I found it difficult to wrap my head around the idea that a king could be thought of as a welcome check on parliamentary power.

"Although Britain did not have a system of checks and balances as strong as the modern American system," O'Shaughnessy responded, "there were nevertheless three parts to the British government: the king, the House of Commons, and the House of Lords. So those were validly seen as some of the checks on the power of each other. That was what they were appealing to," he said, referring to the colonists' petition.

"It was a very curious and late argument being made by Jefferson and other Americans as well—that the king should intervene against Parliament," he continued. "It's bizarre because it really went contrary to their own beliefs. Essentially, the way Jefferson saw the British Empire was as an empire of equals in which the king would act as an umpire, but America would not be formally ruled by Parliament. He denied that had ever been the case. Which was a bit of a stretch—Parliament had been making laws for America for a century. They knew very well that the British regarded the authority of Parliament as critical to their own liberties, as a real check on royal power. So, in a way, it was a last desperate appeal." The Olive Branch Petition, he noted, was the result of an attempt by "the moderates in Congress, who asked the king to intervene and umpire the dispute."

The petition hit London on August 14, 1775. It didn't help the American paceniks' cause that arriving at the same time was a captured letter John Adams had written to a friend in the

Massachusetts Sons of Liberty. Printed in Tory newspapers, Adams's letter complained that the petition "has given a silly Cast to our whole Doings," followed by a promise to ship gunpowder soon.

Adams was right to attack the logic of the petition. Its arguments didn't make much sense, but the motivation behind it did: preventing bloodshed, or at least putting it off. In the dustbin of history, John Dickinson and the moderates come into blurry view mainly as the dithering butts of jokes by official icons like Adams and George Washington, who complained a few days before the Declaration of Independence was signed (though not by the abstaining Dickinson) that the moderates were "still feeding themselves upon the dainty food of reconciliation."

Dickinson was the son and husband of Quakers. Though he was a lapsed Quaker himself, he couldn't help being influenced by that religion's insistence on nonviolence, a doctrine inspired by Jesus's not particularly popular admonitions to "love your enemies" and "turn the other cheek."

Dickinson, who would go on to be one of the framers of the Constitution, was one of the colonial thinkers whose words had inspired the rebellion. As the anonymous author of the influential 1767 essays *Letters from a Farmer in Pennsylvania*, he denounced parliamentary crackdowns against "the liberty of these colonies." To rally the different regions in common cause, he clarified, "I say of these colonies; for the cause of one is the cause of all. If the Parliament may lawfully deprive New York of any of her rights, it may deprive any or all the other colonies of their rights." He did not dismiss the possibility of armed revolt, pointing out, "English history affords frequent examples of resistance by force." However, he cautioned that force "never can be justifiable, until the people are FULLY CONVINCED, that any further submission will be destructive to their happiness." Eight years later, the Olive Branch Petition that Adams found so silly jibed with that cautious creed; Massachusetts was already at war, but Dickinson was still not fully convinced to an all-caps degree.

After Dickinson and Adams had it out over the Olive Branch Petition, Adams wrote to his wife, Abigail, that he and Dickinson "are not to be on speaking terms."

How sad is it that this tiff sort of cheers me up? If two of the most distinguished, dedicated, and thoughtful public servants in the history of this republic could not find a way to agree to disagree, how can we expect the current crop of congressional blockheads to get along?

While the Olive Branch Petition is a useful tool for understanding the depth and sincerity of the rebels' internal disputes, in practical terms it was a complete waste of time. George III refused to even read the thing. On August 23, the king issued "A Proclamation for Suppressing Rebellion and Sedition" in the American colonies, followed by his October address to Parliament calling for "a speedy end to these disorders by the most decisive exertions." He wrote, "For this purpose, I have increased my naval establishment, and greatly augmented my land forces," hastily adding, "but in such a manner as may be the least burthensome to my kingdoms"—because apparently it

ADAMS

had finally dawned on him that sometimes his subjects could get a bit touchy about taxes.

When news of the king's speech reached Massachusetts in November of 1775, Abigail Adams wrote to John, "Let us separate, they are unworthy to be our Brethren. Let us renounce them and instead of supplications as formerly for their prosperity and happiness, Let us beseech the almighty to blast their councils and bring to Nought all their devices."

Of course the finest expression of how the colonists had turned on the king was the Declaration of Independence, approved the following July. Thomas Jefferson singled out George III, proclaiming, "The history of the present King of Great Britain is a history of repeated injuries and usurpations, all having in direct object the establishment of an absolute Tyranny over these States." More important, all of Jefferson's specific digs at the king were preceded by one self-evident fact that obliterated any and all justifications for monarchy, aristocracy, and colonialism until the end of time, even though neither its author nor his comrades truly believed it: *All men are created equal.*

A few true-blue moderates still clung to a futile hope for reconciliation with Britain when Bonvouloir, the French foreign minister's spy, arrived in Philadelphia at the end of 1775. But to any objective observer, much less an Anglophobic Frenchman hoping to chat up Ben Franklin, most colonists' commitment to prolonging the war seemed like a safe bet.

Whether or not they could win was another question. When Bonvouloir enlisted a Frenchman living in Philadelphia to introduce him to Franklin, Franklin feared that the stranger could be a British double agent. However, he was curious and desperate enough to get past these suspicions. Franklin and his fellow Secret Committee member John Jay met with Bonvouloir in Carpenters' Hall on Chestnut Street. Bonvouloir reported back to Vergennes that the Americans were bully for war, over-estimating troop levels of fifty thousand men. (There were less than half that.) Writing to the French ambassador in London, Bonvouloir summed up the patriots' ardor: "The enemy will have to chop them to bits before they will surrender."

In a letter to Vergennes, Bonvouloir reassured the foreign minister that while he had made no promises on behalf of France, the Americans "asked me if France would help them, and at what price. I replied that I believed France *wished them well*" (italics in original).

Consequently, Vergennes was reassured that the Americans were committed to war and that their chances for victory were not entirely hopeless. Also, the Committee of Secret Correspondence shipped Silas Deane to Paris to find out if these French well wishes included things like actual artillery.

Upon receiving this report and reflecting further on Beaumarchais's arguments, in March of 1776 Vergennes sat down and wrote a position paper for Louis XVI he titled "Considerations on the Affairs of the English Colonies in America." "Considered" is the word for this measured, obsequious memo. Vergennes flattered the king, pointing out that Louis was far too wise to get swept up in rash acts of vengeance against Great Britain, even though Britain deserved comeuppance, what with "the evils which since the commencement of the century she has inflicted on those who have had the misfortune to be her neighbors or her rivals."

Vergennes proposed clandestine aid to the rebels to avoid stirring up an overt war with Britain and to shore up the enemy of France's enemy, advising, "The courage of the Americans might be kept up by secret favors and vague hopes." He specifically suggested sending them covert "military stores and money" for the time being but warned against going public and making an official treaty with the insurgents until "the liberty of English America shall have acquired consistency." In other words, they should not stumble into another war with Britain until the Americans prove themselves.

Because these words convinced Louis XVI to open his heart and, more important, his wallet to the patriots, Vergennes's memo arguably had as much practical effect on the establishment of American independence as the Declaration of Independence itself. Jefferson's pretty phrases were incomplete without the punctuation of French gunpowder.

That said, the clairvoyant counterargument France's comptroller general of finance offered to Louis XVI is a far more riveting read. Anne-Robert-Jacques Turgot had had some success in reducing France's budget deficit by slashing government spending. But he was increasingly unpopular among all social classes for some of his other innovative ideas, including his desire to tax the traditionally untaxed aristocracy, his brainstorm about replacing the power of skilled laborers' guilds with a free market approach, and his monkeying with grain pricing during bad harvests that sparked the "flour wars," for which he was, justifiably or not, blamed.

While the foreign minister Vergennes understood the value of wasting a few paragraphs stroking the king's ego before coaxing the king into doing his bidding, Turgot's blunt missives to Louis tended to include rash insults, such as "You are too young to judge men and you have yourself said, Sire, that you lack experience and need a guide." In fact, Turgot's memo on the English colonies in America was his last state document. Having alienated the king, the aristocracy, the middle classes, and the poor, Turgot was forced to resign.

It seems obvious that the economist in charge of bandaging France's bleeding finances would oppose the French monarch's spending money he didn't have to help out some transatlantic anti-monarchist punks. But Turgot's message recommending the king steer clear of the American rebellion is fascinating because it is levelheaded, openhearted, and eerily prophetic all at once.

Turgot was friends with the *philosophes* like Diderot and Voltaire and even contributed anonymous articles on existence and etymology to the great group project of the French Enlightenment, the *Encyclopedia*. After his postwar diplomatic stint in Paris, Thomas Jefferson, an admirer of Turgot's writings on economic theory, would lug home a bust of Turgot, along with those of Voltaire and Lafayette, to display at Monticello.

The reasons Turgot rejected helping the Americans still bear the stamp and sympathies of the Age of Reason. He predicted that colonial independence in general was inevitable and just, especially American independence, remarking on the patriots, "Their will can never be broken."

He went on to speculate that all mother countries that continued to exploit and oppress their colonies would someday "see their colonies escape them all the same, and become their enemies instead of remaining their allies." (This is, for instance, exactly what would happen to the French in 1954 at the battle of Dien Bien Phu, when Viet Minh revolutionaries defeated French forces in northwestern Vietnam, the beginning of the end of French rule in Indochina.)

Turgot also had nothing but respect for the "prudence" of the American leadership, especially Franklin, commending "the enlightenment diffused among them." He even had the foresight to envision postwar stability, anticipating that the rebels would "give a solid form to their government, and that consequently they will love peace and seek to preserve it."

However, as Turgot noted: "The king knows the situation of his finances." There was, for starters, a budget deficit of twenty million livres. "By making premature use of our strength," he said, referring to sending weapons and whatnot to the Americans, "we risk the perpetuating of our weakness," meaning the financial weakness of the national debt, which a few years later would saddle the king's wife, Marie Antoinette, with the nickname "Madame Deficit." France would go on to spend more than one billion livres on the Americans.

Just as he was dead-on about the eventual stability of America's postwar government and the dangers of colonial powers ignoring colonists' understandable desire for independence,

Turgot turned out to be correct regarding this chilling prophecy: "War we ought to shun as the greatest of evils, since it will render impossible for a very long time, and perhaps forever, the reform which is absolutely necessary for the prosperity of the State and for the relief of the people."

In other words, every cent the French government spent on guns for the Americans was another centime it would not have to spend on butter for the starving peasants who would one day storm Versailles.

The best place to mull over Turgot's unheeded warnings is Paris, in the cold marble silence of the Chapelle Expiatoire (Chapel of Atonement). Its domed sanctuary, built over the mass grave where Louis and Marie Antoinette and hundreds of other casualties of the guillotine were buried, was conceived in the monarchs' honor. After the revolution, the king and queen were eventually dug up and reinterred in the traditional royal resting place at Saint-Denis, but the other remains remain, including a mistress of Louis XV and the assassin Charlotte Corday. While the chapel is cool and quiet and built in a Napoleonic neoclassical style my teenage nephew would categorize as "classy," it is one of the few places in Gay Paree where a visitor can stand still and absorb the gravity and barbarity of what happened there, picturing the heaps of skull-less skeletons beneath her feet. Staring at the floor, I thought of the Parisian protesters' whimsical slogan of May 1968: *Under the cobblestones, the beach.* The Chapelle Expiatoire represents the grim archaeological truth: under the marble, the bones.

At least for his efforts on behalf of Americans, the foreign minister Vergennes got a town in Vermont named after him. All Louis XVI got was his head chopped off.

Once Louis XVI agreed to Vergennes's proposal to secretly back the Americans, Vergennes assigned Beaumarchais to solve how to do it without the British finding out. The playwright scripted a scheme in which the king would pay Beaumarchais to set up a fake company under a false identity and use half the money to buy the government's surplus weapons and other equipment gathering dust from the Seven Years' War (in other words, use the king's money to pay the king for his own stuff). Then Beaumarchais proposed to lend the other half of the money to the Americans, who would use it to buy more surplus French equipment from the dummied-up business and hopefully repay the loan with tobacco and other American exports. To throw off the English, the goods could be transferred via the French colonies in the Caribbean if need be, and no one other than the king, the foreign minister, and the playwright would know the whole truth. The king was so amused by the kooky plan, he decided to convince his cousin the king of Spain to pitch in as well.

"We are secretly giving you a million francs," Vergennes informed Beaumarchais. "We shall get Spain to contribute an equal sum." Thus Beaumarchais gave his phony business a Spanish name, Rodrige Hortalez & Company. In June of 1776, Vergennes issued the promised million francs to the fictional Spaniard's firm, a sum doubled a few weeks later when Spanish matching funds arrived. Beaumarchais rented an elaborate office in the Marais district of Paris, though he was obviously the only one who ever laid eyes on the illusive "Monsieur Hortalez."

When my friend Steven and I went looking for the building one afternoon, we came to the address at 47 rue Vieille-du-Temple and realized we had been there before. Steven scrolled through his phone to show me the photo he had taken on a previous trip of me standing in front of the former Rodrigue Hortalez & Company portal, sticking out my tongue to mimic the intricately carved tongue-wagging figure on the door. I wonder if Beaumarchais smiled every time he passed by the smart-alecky carving before going inside and performing both parts of loud, hammy conversations with "Monsieur Hortalez" behind closed doors.

When Silas Deane showed up at Versailles in July of 1776 asking Vergennes to secretly supply the Americans when Vergennes had just passed along money to Beaumarchais to secretly supply the Americans, Vergennes smiled and shooed Deane away from his office lest the English get wind. He then dispatched Beaumarchais to Deane's doorstep to inform the congressional representative that clandestine help would soon be on the way.

As Beaumarchais began to track down cannons and cannonballs, that August an ominous and unprecedented British armada of 450 ships and boats carrying forty-five thousand British soldiers and sailors, as well as the rented Germanic troops known as the Hessians (of Headless Horseman fame), assembled in New York Harbor under the command of the sib-

VERGENNES

lings Admiral Lord Richard "Black Dick" Howe and his little brother General Sir William Howe. One eyewitness in New York City marveled that the waterfront was so overstuffed with terrifying British vessels, saying, "I declare I thought all London was afloat."

As Beaumarchais gathered blankets and grenades in France, William Howe's redcoats came ashore and slaughtered Washington's forces on Long Island, in Brooklyn, and then in Manhattan. A humiliated Washington could do nothing to stop his troops' shoddy retreat from Kips Bay, swatting at them with his horsewhip and howling, "Are these the men with which I am to defend America?"

They skedaddled north, only to lose the Battle of White Plains in Westchester County. Then on November 16, from across the Hudson River, Washington watched the fall of his namesake Fort Washington, the last American refuge in Manhattan, delivering unto the enemy nearly three thousand American prisoners of war in a single afternoon. New York City was lost for the rest of the war. Manhattan was not only the British headquarters and naval base for the next seven years; its waterfront was also the home of the diabolical prison ships in which skeletal POWs resorted to eating the lice off their skin once they ran out of rats. Nearly twelve thousand of them perished of disease and malnutrition—more than died in combat at all the actual battles of the war combined.

By December, Beaumarchais's muskets, tents, and shovels, not to mention nearly three hundred thousand pounds of gunpowder, were piling up promisingly in French ports—

unbeknownst to the miserable, beaten-down patriot troops huddled around New Jersey listening to Thomas Paine's new pamphlet *The American Crisis* being read aloud. It began, "These are the times that try men's souls."

Beaumarchais went incognito to the port of Le Havre to oversee his top-secret cargo being loaded onto ships. He arrived under an assumed name, planning to keep a low profile. That is, until he discovered the local thespians botching a production of *The Barber of Seville*. Enraged at the lame state of his play, Beaumarchais unmasked himself and demanded to start running rehearsals, going back and forth from the docks to the theater, barking at actors and stevedores alike.

When my playwright friend Sherm and I see a reproduction of one of the cannons sent by Beaumarchais on view at Monmouth Battlefield State Park, I question Beaumarchais's priorities. That he blew his cover as an arms dealer to tweak a provincial production makes perfect sense to Sherm, though. His only concern for his fellow dramatist is, "How did that production of *The Barber of Seville* turn out once he'd tinkered with it?"

The British were well aware of Beaumarchais's plot because their secret agent Edward Bancroft had gotten the handy job of being Silas Deane's secretary in Paris. But the Brits could not act on this intel without exposing their valuable inside man. That is, until London heard from its other spies in Le Havre about the Beaumarchais shenanigans. The British government immediately made a stink to the French government, threatening war. Louis XVI was forced to pretend ignorance and order

Beaumarchais to stand down and cancel the shipments to America. Luckily for the Americans, Beaumarchais got word this order was on its way, and the largest of his three ships was already crossing the Atlantic by the time Beaumarchais received the king's command.

Meanwhile, back in New Jersey, on December 27, 1776, a gloating George Washington sent the congressional president John Hancock a letter that began, "Sir, I have the pleasure of congratulating you upon the Success of an Enterprize." The enterprise in question involved Washington leading his troops across the icy Delaware River on Christmas night and springing a sneak attack at dawn on Hessian troops encamped at Trenton.

It was a bold and tricky maneuver and one of Washington's greatest achievements as a tactician and commander. Relieved to be delivering the first good news in months, Washington informed Hancock that the enemy "finding . . . that they were surrounded, and that they must inevitably be cut to pieces if they made any further Resistance, they agreed to lay down their Arms." He lauded the valor of his troops, remarking, "Their Behaviour upon this Occasion, reflects the highest honor upon them." He noted that while he had lost a "trifling" three or four men, he was suddenly in possession of nearly nine hundred prisoners of war, including, if genealogy shows on cable TV are to be believed, the Hessian great-something-grandfather of actor Rob Lowe.

The victory at Trenton boosted morale among the troops, the Congress, and the people to a degree possibly unwarranted by winning back a town in New Jersey, what with it being a town in New Jersey. Nevertheless, news that the Continentals had gotten the drop on a few hundred napping Germans alerted a skeptical world that Washington and his scrappy losers might perhaps, possibly, maybe have a shot at winning.

By the time the Trenton update reached France, Benjamin Franklin had arrived in Paris. He, Silas Deane, and Arthur Lee were working together (sort of—Lee and Deane never managed to get along). According to the letter the three sent to Congress, the Trenton victory "produced the most vivid sensation" in France. "The hearts of the French people are universally for us and the opinion for an immediate war with Great Britain is very strong," they boasted. But they also warned, "The court has its reasons for postponing a little longer." Putting off *official* entry into the war, they meant, given that securing an open and official alliance with the French was the reason Franklin had showed up in France.

At least the good news from New Jersey emboldened Vergennes to allow Beaumarchais to send off more cargo-laden ships—which would eventually total forty. On March 17, 1777, the first of them arrived and dropped anchor in Portsmouth, New Hampshire. A Philadelphia newspaper soon reported, "By an express from the eastward we are informed, that a vessel is just arrived from France with 12,000 stands of arms, besides a large quantity of powder and clothes."

While the shipment cheered up the rebels, the various commanders in various places started jockeying for supplies willynilly. Washington wrote to Congress to make the rather obvious suggestion that "the disposal and direction of Military Stores should be only with one body or one person. At present this power is exercised thro' so many Channels, that much confusion is introduced." On the one hand, what an embarrassment that two years into the war the rebels had not gotten around to setting up an efficient system for managing and dispersing supplies. On the other hand, actually having supplies to disperse was a new problem Washington was probably happy to have.

By the end of April, the *Boston Gazette* announced the arrival of another French ship bearing fifty-eight cannons, enough clothing and tents for ten thousand men, and ten tons of powder, as well as "a colonel and twenty-four officers."

Lafayette was far from the only European soldier of rank aspiring to join the Continental Army. Deane had asked Beaumarchais for help in recruiting experienced warriors, especially engineers to beef up fortifications and artillery specialists to operate the cannons and mortars being shipped. Deane assured Beaumarchais that Congress would pay back the cash signing bonuses the playwright doled out to the men. (Congress never did reimburse Beaumarchais for any of his expenses. According to his biographer Harlow Giles Unger, in 1835, nearly four decades after the playwright's death, Congress finally offered his heirs about a third of what he was owed—eight hundred thousand francs, or roughly three million dollars in today's money.)

Among the officers Beaumarchais recruited and/or shipped to America were all-stars of the Revolution such as the Polish count and "father of American cavalry" Casimir Pulaski, the Prussian officer Friedrich Wilhelm von Steuben (whose drills at

Valley Forge transformed Washington's peasants with pitch-forks into a professional army), and the architect and engineer Pierre L'Enfant, who stuck around after the war to design the plan of Washington, DC. But these future national treasures were the exception, not the rule.

With Europe temporarily at peace and France in particular cutting military spending in light of its budget deficit, Deane complained of being "well-nigh harassed to death with applications of officers to go to America." One of them even wanted George Washington's job, and Deane was not opposed to giving it to him. "My aim is simply to find a man whose name and reputation alone will demoralize the enemy. Such a man is available, and I believe I have found him," Deane wrote to Congress. He added, "The question is to win his confidence, which can only be done by heaping sufficient honors upon him to gratify his ambition, as, for instance, naming him commander-in-chief." Even accounting for Washington's thumping in the New York campaign, this was a tacky, literally un-American plan. The scheme was obviously thwarted, but interestingly enough, the Frenchman conniving to steal Washington's job was none other than Lafayette's old commanding officer, the Comte de Broglie, though Lafayette was ignorant of the plot.

Congress was soon neck-deep in arrogant boobs whom Beaumarchais or Deane had promised high ranks and higher salaries. "Men cannot be engaged to quit their native country . . . in a cause which is not their own" is how Deane rationalized the incentives to Congress.

Lafayette and his two best friends from the Noailles Regiment, his brother-in-law the Vicomte de Noailles and the Comte de Ségur, were keen to sign up. "We were tired of the *longeur* of the peace that had lasted ten years," Ségur recalled, "and each of us burned with a desire to repair the affronts of the last wars, to fight the English and to fly to help the American cause."

Lafayette met Silas Deane through Johann de Kalb, a Bavarian-born French officer and a veteran of the Seven Years' War. Lafayette wrote, "When I presented to Mr. Deane my boyish face, (for I was scarcely nineteen years of age), I spoke more of my ardor in the cause than of my experience." And if all-purpose gusto wasn't enough of a selling point, Lafayette "dwelt much upon the effect my departure would excite in France, and he signed our mutual agreement."

Unlike the orphan Lafayette, his friends Ségur and Noailles asked their families' permission to leave, which is how the king, Vergennes, and, worst of all, Lafayette's father-in-law, Jean de Noailles, found out about their plans. Rumors that three such highborn military blue bloods were preparing to fight the English in America threatened to aggravate the international incident whipped up by Beaumarchais. The three boys were expressly forbidden from going. In fact, to placate the English, Louis XVI publicly banned all French soldiers from volunteering in America. The foreign minister Vergennes notified the Paris police that officers or infantrymen intent on sailing to America were to be arrested "with plenty of publicity and severity." As an act of damage control, Vergennes even held his nose and sent the British ambassador to France a nice phony note congratulating him on "the happy news of the successes of the British arms" in New York.

Once word of the losses in New York arrived in France, Deane gave Lafayette an out on going through with his plans. "I called upon Mr. Deane," Lafayette recalled, "and I thanked him for his frankness. 'Until now, sir,' said I, 'you have only seen my ardor in your cause, and that may not prove at present wholly useless." Lafayette reassured Deane that he was still resolute about going to America: "I shall purchase a ship to carry out your officers; we must feel confidence in the future." Must we? Even a cool customer like Washington was said to have wept when he watched Fort Washington fall. Confidence was not a rational response to the debacle of the New York campaign. But Lafayette not only sent a guy to Bordeaux to buy a twenty-two-ton ship; he also had it renamed *La Victoire*, i.e., the *Victory*.

Not until Theodore Roosevelt resigned his prestigious position as assistant secretary of the navy in 1898 to fight with the Rough Riders in the Cuban dirt would there be a rich man as weirdly rabid to join American forces in combat as Lafayette was. The two shared a child's ideal of manly military glory. Though in Lafayette's defense, he was an actual teenager, unlike the thirty-nine-year-old TR.

Looking back on Lafayette's biography, a few incidents foreshadow what a headstrong pill he would be about absconding to America, such as foiling his father-in-law's attempt to get him hired by the king's brother. The words Lafayette used to describe that triumph—"I did not hesitate to be disagreeable to preserve my independence"—applied to getting his way regarding America as well. Perhaps the most emblematic anecdote foretelling Lafayette's stubborn refusal to give up his American dream was the boyhood story about how one day, one of his Parisian schoolteachers was talking up the virtues of an obedient horse. According to Lafayette, "I described the perfect horse as one which, at the sight of the whip, had the sense to throw his rider to the ground before he could be whipped."

And so, bucking the king's orders and his father-in-law's admonitions, Lafayette pretended to drop the idea of dashing off to America, all the while furtively planning his getaway. As he described his deceptions, "The secrecy with which this negotiation and my preparations were made appears almost a miracle; family, friends, ministers; French spies and English spies, all were kept completely in the dark as to my intentions."

Perhaps his most bratty act of misdirection was to bop over to London for a previously scheduled visit to his father-in-law's uncle, the French ambassador to Great Britain. Ambassador Noailles trotted out Lafayette at various parties and social functions, including the opera, where the boy bumped into General Sir Henry Clinton, future commander in chief of the British army in America.

"While I concealed my intentions," Lafayette admitted of his time in London, "I openly avowed my sentiments; I often defended the Americans; I rejoiced at their success at Trenton"—news of which had just arrived. A clueless Ambassador Noailles even presented Lafayette to King George III, a courtesy that would prove plenty embarrassing to the diplomat once Lafayette escaped to the colonies. Later on, Lafayette would blame this mischief on his youth, conceding that he was "too fond of playing a trick upon the king he is going to fight with."

Without a word to Noailles, Lafayette skipped town and crept back to France, but not to his in-laws' home. He hid out with Kalb outside Paris, and then the two made their way to Bordeaux and the *Victory*.

Lafayette's family found his goodbye letters after he was gone. "You will be astonished, my dear papa," he wrote to his father-in-law, "by what I am about to tell you. I am a general officer in the army of the United States of America." He was right—Jean de Noailles was flabbergasted and enraged. Ditto the king, Vergennes, and the rest of the royal cabinet. An embarrassed Ambassador Noailles wrote to the French prime minister Maurepas from London, "Fortunately his age may excuse his thoughtlessness." Maurepas nevertheless described Lafayette's flight as "a hostile act." Though the aforementioned authority figures were more than justified in being miffed with Lafayette, the person with the most cause for contempt was Adrienne, Lafayette's knocked-up teenage wife.

In the letter Lafayette left for Adrienne, he confessed, "I am too guilty to vindicate myself. Do not be angry with me. Believe that I am sorely distressed." He asked her to "embrace our Henriette," their two-year-old, adding that Adrienne's pregnancy "adds to my torment. If you knew how painful this is . . ."

Lafayette's note to Adrienne follows the same callous template as the one George Washington addressed to his wife, Martha, after he agreed to become the commander in chief of the Continental Army. Martha burned their letters upon George's death to preserve their privacy, but the one from June 18, 1775, survived because it was stuffed in a desk drawer and forgotten. "I should enjoy more real happiness and felicity in one month with you, at home, than I have the most distant prospect of reaping abroad," he whimpered. At least Washington could point out to his middle-aged spouse that he was chosen for this duty, acknowledging, "It has been a kind of destiny that has thrown me upon this Service." Lafayette, on the other hand, was more of a make-your-own-destiny type of fellow, disobeying orders from the king and abandoning a pregnant girl for an entirely optional adventure.

"I was with child, and I loved him dearly," Adrienne wrote. "My father and the rest of the family were all in a violent rage at the news." While Lafayette's father-in-law was ratting him out to Versailles, his mother-in-law got stuck with notifying her preggers daughter. As Adrienne recalled, "She brought the painful news of his cruel departure to me herself and tried to console me." While her father was egging on the government to send men to hunt down Lafayette and drag him home, her mother tried to look on the bright side of her son-in-law's perhaps idealistic antics. Adrienne wrote, "She had no knowledge of great quests or glory, but predicted two years before everyone else that Lafayette would achieve both."

Before the *Victory* put out from Bordeaux, Lafayette received bleak news from home. "The anger of the government" gave

ADRIENNE LAFAYETTE

him pause, especially orders to report forthwith to the French military barracks in Marseilles. "The letters from my family were terrible," he wrote. "They forbade my going to America . . . They reminded me of the grief I was causing my pregnant, loving wife."

He nevertheless set sail, but as the ship headed south along the coast, the guilt ate at him. When the ship docked in Spain, Lafayette left his mates, including a furious Kalb, to wait there while he rode back to France to make amends—sort of.

Back in Bordeaux, Lafayette once again received orders to report to Marseilles, and he wrote to Prime Minister Maurepas asking for a reversal on the royal order banning his trip to America. Meanwhile, Kalb informed the Comte de Broglie that he and the other enlistees on the *Victory* were stalled in Spain waiting for Lafayette to either return or release them. Broglie was (unbeknownst to Lafayette) counting on Kalb to convince the Continental Congress to hire him to replace George Washington. Thus the old man was anxious for Kalb to get going. To that end, Broglie sent an aide to Bordeaux to cajole Lafayette with a fib about how the royal order was all a big show meant to humor Lafayette's father-in-law and how the French government was secretly cheering him on. Since this hooey was exactly what Lafayette wanted to hear, he happily chose to believe it. He then wrote the prime minister a ridiculous follow-up note claiming that since he had not received a reply to his request to lift the command to remain in France, he considered the minister's "silence was a tacit order" to proceed to America.

Since tacit orders couldn't exactly be handed over to the

men chasing him, Lafayette pretended to head to Marseilles per the official orders. He then disguised himself in a courier's getup, made a U-turn for Spain, and sweet-talked an innkeeper's daughter he had flirted with en route to point his trackers in the wrong direction.

How did adults understand teenage hijinks like this before neuroscientists discovered that a human's prefrontal cortex—the part of the brain responsible for planning, evaluating risk, and considering consequences—is not fully developed until around age twenty-five? I bet the nineteen-year-old Lafayette's infuriated father-in-law might have had more empathy for the boy's half-baked decisions if he could have watched a couple of segments of that *Frontline* episode "Inside the Teenage Brain." When a kid practicing tricks at a skateboard ramp explains he doesn't wear a helmet because "it's not that risky," the documentary's narrator deadpans, "Well, 'not *that* risky' would be one way to put it."

The clumsy slapstick of Lafayette's exodus concluded on April 20, 1777, when he finally shipped out from Spain. On the eve of his exit he posted a gloomy note to Adrienne, pledging, "My heart is broken. Tomorrow is the moment of cruel departure."

At least there was a kind of symmetry in Adrienne enduring morning sickness alone in Paris while seasickness was smiting her deadbeat husband across the Atlantic. He spent the miserable voyage learning English, presumably mastering how to conjugate the verb "to puke." While on board, he complained in a letter to Adrienne, "The sea is so melancholy, that we mutually, I believe, sadden each other." The enthusiastically named *Victory* had become "the most wearisome of all human habitations."

At sea, he unveiled the grandeur of his mission to Adrienne and attempted to include her in it. He wrote, "I hope that as a favor to me you will become a good American." He really wasn't in a position to ask her for favors, especially this baffling request for a Parisian aristocrat to somehow live by New World republican principles in her mansion in the old regime.

Lafayette proclaimed to his wife, "The welfare of America is intimately bound up with the happiness of humanity. She is going to become the deserving and sure refuge of virtue, of honesty, of tolerance, of equality, and of a tranquil liberty."

To establish such a forthright dreamland of decency, who wouldn't sign up to shoot at a few thousand Englishmen, just as long as Mr. Bean wasn't one of them? Alas, from my end of history there's a big file cabinet blocking the view of the sweet-natured republic Lafayette foretold, and it's where the guvment keeps the folders full of Indian treaties, the Chinese Exclusion Act, and NSA-monitored electronic messages pertinent to national security, which is apparently all of them, including the one in which I ask my mom for advice on how to get a red Sharpie stain out of couch upholstery.

Lafayette confided to his wife, "In coming as a friend to offer my services to this intriguing republic, I bring to it only my frankness and my good will; no ambition, no self-interest; in working for my glory, I work for their happiness." Disregarding the inherent contradictions of proclaiming his lack of ambition and self-interest in the same sentence, he revealed that attaining glory was one of his two stated goals. The phrase "coming as a friend" glows on the page because it turned out to be the truth.

It's appropriate to ding Lafayette for the casual cruelty with which he abandoned his family, roll the eyes a bit at his retro quest for fame, or envy his outlandish optimism. But none of that negates the fact that he turned out to be the best friend America ever had. And I am not only referring to his youthful derring-do on battlegrounds up and down the Eastern Seaboard. I am also referring to any number of his dull grown-up kindnesses later on, such as assisting Thomas Jefferson, the United States minister to France in the 1780s, in opening up French markets to American goods. Lafayette's lobbying procured Nantucket whalers the contract to supply the whale oil that lit the streetlights of Paris. Because of Lafayette, the City of Lights glowed by New England's boiled blubber. And to say thanks for getting them the gig, all Nantucket rallied its milk cows to send him a giant wheel of cheese. When Lafayette visited Monticello in 1824, his old friend Thomas Jefferson toasted him: "When I was stationed in his country for the purpose of cementing its friendship with ours, and of advancing our mutual interests, this friend of both, was my most powerful auxiliary and advocate. He made our cause his own . . . His influence and connections there were great. All doors of all departments were open to him at all times. In truth, I only held the nail, he drove it."

Finally, after Lafayette had spent two months on the *Victory* "floating on this dreary plain"—land ho. Lafayette, Kalb, and a few men came ashore north of Charleston around midnight on June 13, 1777, waking up the household of Major Benjamin Huger of the South Carolina militia. Huger put them up. "I retired to rest that night rejoicing that I had at last attained the haven of my dreams," Lafayette recalled. He went on to gush, "The next morning was beautiful. Everything around me was new to me, the room, the bed draped in delicate mosquito curtains, the black servants who came to me quietly to ask my commands, the strange new beauty of the landscape outside my windows, the luxuriant vegetation—all combined to produce a magical effect."

In other words, it was a buggy swamp chock-full of slaves. But Lafayette was a man in love. He proceeded to Charleston, and of course Charleston was the tops, "one of the best built, handsomest, and most agreeable cities that I have ever seen." After hobnobbing with local luminaries, including Continental Congress delegate John Rutledge, Lafayette wrote to his wife, "All the persons with whom I wished to be acquainted have shewn me the greatest attention and politeness (not European politeness merely)."

Charleston's embrace inspired him to report, "What delights me most is that all citizens are brothers." Then again, he was mostly hanging out with other Masons. The only Carolinians that failed to captivate him had wings. "I am devoured by gnats covering me with big bites," he wrote.

Lafayette paid for four carriages and a few horses to ferry him, Kalb, and the other French officers north. They left

Charleston on June 25. According to the diary of one of the officers, Charles-François du Buysson, "Four days later, some of our carriages were reduced to splinters; several of the horses which were old and unsteady were either worn out or lame." Lafayette, a good sport, quipped to Adrienne, "I set out in a brilliant manner in a carriage, and I must now tell you that we are all on horseback, having broken the carriage . . . and I hope soon to write you that we have arrived on foot."

As they spent the next month trudging north toward Pennsylvania via North Carolina, Virginia, Maryland, and Delaware, Lafayette delighted in the way "vast forests and immense rivers combine to give to that country an appearance of youth and majesty."

Du Buysson, on the other hand, complained, "We traveled a great part of the way on foot, often sleeping in the woods, almost dead with hunger, exhausted by the heat, several of us suffering from fever and from dysentery." Lafayette downplayed the hardships, reporting to Adrienne, "There have been some fatigues; but, although a few of my companions have suffered from them, I have scarcely noticed them."

The American people, he wrote, "are as amiable as my enthusiasm led me to imagine." He fawned, "Simplicity of manners, a desire to oblige . . . a sweet equality reign here among everybody." Which was, in 1777, the kind of thing only a white guy could say. Still, Lafayette's delight in New World hospitality rings true. While there are many reasons to visit France, warmth is not necessarily one of them. I once complained to a Parisian acquaintance how her city's mania for exact change can be off-putting for a traveler, what with getting yelled at by cashiers and cab drivers all day long for the crime of paying a sixteen-euro fare with a twenty-euro note. She said that it was nothing personal, that the French are naturally aggressive, especially with one another. Which I suppose is a form of equality, but not the sweet kind experienced by Lafayette.

At least one of Lafayette's traveling companions would have happily traded American friendliness for French infrastructure. "At last, after thirty-two days of marching, we arrived in Philadelphia," Du Buysson wrote. "I think I am safe in saying that in Europe, no campaign would be harder to go through than was this journey."

After disappointing his wife and offending her family, being chased across France by government henchmen, vomiting his way across the Atlantic, and hiking through six humid states, Lafayette was anticipating some sort of congressional attaboy. They all were. According to Du Buysson, "We were encouraged by the bright prospect of the reception we counted upon from the people there." Alas, what they got was a brusque dismissal from a congressional grouch.

"The moment," Lafayette recalled, "was peculiarly unfavourable to strangers. The Americans were displeased with the pretensions, and disgusted with the conduct, of many Frenchmen." Consequently, he wrote, "the Congress finally adopted the plan of not listening to any stranger."

So when Lafayette and friends called at the State House (then the moniker of Independence Hall), Congressman James Lovell of Massachusetts shooed them away, snarling, "It seems that French officers have a great fancy to enter our service without being invited."

In fact, most of them, including Lafayette, had been invited—by Beaumarchais or Silas Deane. Hence the throngs of irksome Frenchmen who had been washing ashore for months, expecting to be welcomed with rank and riches.

While the Continental Army was always in need of fresh meat, it needed more men who could follow orders, as opposed to giving them, and preferably in English. Factors ranging from smallpox to enlisted men declining to reenlist at the end of their tours undermined troop strength. In fact, just as Lafayette was on the road between Charleston and Philadelphia, Washington wrote a letter admitting it was "very unlikely that any effectual opposition can be given to the British Army with the Troops we have, whose Numbers diminish more by desertion than Increas'd by Inlistments."

Even so, Washington had no interest in driving up his numbers with the influx of European dilettantes, complaining, "These men have no attachment nor ties to the country."

Back in February, when Lafayette was still moseying around London, Washington ranted to Congress about the Frenchmen, "This evil, if I may call it so, is a growing one; for, from what I learn, they are coming in swarms from old France." Washington deplored their "ignorance of our language" and pointed out that American officers "would be disgusted if foreigners were put over their heads."

Which was exactly what happened upon the arrival of one Philippe du Coudray, a French veteran of the Seven Years' War who turned up in Philadelphia a month before Lafayette. Silas Deane had been hoodwinked by Du Coudray's padded résumé, believing him to be a nobleman well connected at the court of Louis XVI and France's greatest living artillery hotshot, when he was, in actuality, a wine merchant's son who had seen a few cannons. Deane, who wasn't exactly god's gift to human resources, as the Continental Congress was slowly figuring out, promised Du Coudray the rank of major general and command of the army's artillery corps and engineers.

Turns out that replacing the Continental Army's beloved chief artillery officer, Henry Knox, was not as easy and arbitrary as *Bewitched* casting a second Darrin. Henry Knox *was* the revolution.

Born in Boston in 1759 to Irish immigrants, Knox dropped out of school to support his mother and siblings after his father's death, apprenticing as a bookbinder and working as a clerk in a bookstore. He saved enough money by the time he was twenty-one to open his own establishment, the London Book Store.

All Bostonians suffered in the wake of the Coercive Acts of 1774, shopkeepers especially. To rebuke the renegades who had dressed up like Indians and plunked crates of the East India Company's tea into Boston Harbor, Parliament passed the punitive laws colonists referred to as the Intolerable Acts—including the Boston Port Act that closed the harbor. The troublemakers were supposed to reimburse the East India Company for its drowned merchandise and the crown for its lost tax revenue.

The port closure gummed up international trade, affecting many Bostonians' livelihoods, including bookseller Knox, who

KNOX

depended on book shipments from the British capital for which he named his shop. Plus, locals were boycotting British goods out of spite anyway. In November of 1774, Knox wrote to a London bookseller to whom he owed money, "I had the fairest prospect of entirely balancing our account this fall, but the almost total stagnation of Trade in consequence of the Boston Port Bill has been the sole means of preventing it." He added that the patriots' boycott compounded his woes, complaining, "Now the nonconsumption agreement will stop that small circulation of Business left."

Meant to slap Massachusetts into submission and serve as a warning to the other colonies, the Intolerable Acts backfired, further radicalizing an already radical Massachusetts and rallying the other colonies to come to its material and political aid. In fact, they started calling themselves the United Colonies, sent food to Massachusetts, and convened the First Continental Congress to mull over the mother country's increasingly oppressive policies.

A humble, bootstrappy patriot, Knox wooed, then married Lucy Flucker, the highbrow daughter of the Loyalist governor of the province of Massachusetts. Praised by John Adams for his "inquisitive turn of mind," Knox began preparing for the coming war by reading as many military books as he could find (especially those devoted to ordnance and fortifications), observing redcoat maneuvers around town, quizzing the soldiers who patronized his shop, and joining a local militia, the Boston Grenadiers.

Shots fired in Lexington and Concord on April 19, 1775, had Knox leaving his faltering shop in his little brother's care and rowing to Cambridge with his wife, Lucy (who sewed his sword into the lining of her coat), to throw in with the gathering New England militias.

Things could have been worse. The militias technically lost the Battle of Bunker Hill in June, but they fought with so much heart and inflicted such heavy casualties on the redcoats that British general Thomas Gage wrote home to the secretary of state for the colonies, "The rebels are not the despicable rabble too many have supposed them to be," concluding "that the conquest of this Country is not easy."

"Despicable rabble," however, pretty much summed up George Washington's opinion of the troops when he arrived in Cambridge in July. In a letter to his brother John, the new commander in chief grumbled, "I found a mixed multitude of People here, under very little discipline, order, or Government."

Both Gage and Washington turned out to be correct: the newly minted Continental Army's men didn't always know what they were doing, but they would prove difficult to beat.

Publicly, Washington issued orders to the men "that all Distinctions of Colonies will be laid aside; so that one and the same spirit may animate the whole." Privately, to a fellow Virginian, he despaired of "an unaccountable kind of stupidity in the lower class of these people which, believe me, prevails but too generally among the officers of the Massachusetts part of the Army." So much for that jazz Lafayette was going on about all Americans being brothers.

As Washington tried to deal with a dangerous shortage of gunpowder and an overabundance of smallpox and drunkenness among the men, one of the few bright spots of his arrival in Massachusetts was making the acquaintance of the neither drunk nor stupid Henry Knox.

Knox wrote to his wife that once Washington surveyed the homemade fortifications Knox had erected in Boston's environs, the general "expressed the greatest pleasure and surprise at their situation and apparent utility."

The British occupied the peninsula of Boston, and their navy controlled the harbor, resupplying the city with provisions shipped down from Canada. But the patriots had them surrounded and had been keeping the city under siege for months. To break the stalemate, the Continentals needed bigger, better guns. The good news from Lake Champlain was that Ethan Allen's Green Mountain Boys, with an assist from Benedict Arnold, had captured Fort Ticonderoga and its cache of cannons, mortars, and howitzers. The bad news was that the fort was nearly three hundred miles away, and the problem with heavy artillery is that it's kind of heavy.

Enter Henry Knox. The twenty-five-year-old bookworm approached Washington and volunteered to go to Fort Ticonderoga to fetch the equipment. Washington approved the cockamamie mission. And so, that November Knox and his brother set off for New York. Who knew they would return in January with forty-three cannons, fourteen mortars, and two howitzers dragged across frozen rivers and over the snowy Berkshire Mountains by oxen on custom sleds. This is the derivation of that old Yankee proverb that if you can sell a book, you can move sixty tons of weaponry three hundred miles in winter.

The crafty Washington had the guns dragged up the hills of Dorchester Heights in the middle of the night. When the British and Loyalist Americans ensconced in Boston woke up on March 6, 1776, they were shocked to see the scary fruits of Knox's labor pointing down in their direction. "My God," marveled the British general William Howe, "these fellows have done more work in one night than I could make my army do in three months."

With the forecast calling for a heavy rain of cannonballs, on March 17 the redcoats and the Loyalist townsfolk promptly hightailed it out of Boston by ships bound for Nova Scotia. (Including Knox's Tory in-laws—Lucy Knox never saw her family again.) In a grim report to Lord George Germain, secretary of state for America, Howe admitted to "there not being the least prospect of conciliating this continent until its armies shall have been roughly dealt with," adding, "I confess my apprehensions that such an event will not be readily brought about."

While the triumph in Boston was not a particularly representative episode in the long war, it does bear the closest resemblance to the stories we tell ourselves about the Revolution. It was opry defeats opera, a model of DIY Yankee pluck. A patchwork of amateur militias made up of barely trained farmers, lawyers, shopkeepers, and artisans who, thanks to a hometown book nerd's folkloric stunt, drove some of earth's most experienced professional warriors out of a long-suffering city.

So, the moral of that story, other than never underestimate

an independent bookseller, was that the Continental Army and its commander in chief had a soft spot for Chief Artillery Officer Henry Knox. It's poetic that the Kentucky fort protecting the United States Bullion Depository was named after him: for Washington, Henry Knox was money in the bank.

Hence the group flip-out the following year when Congress instructed Washington to hand over command of the artillery corps—composed of men recruited and trained by Knox—to the newly arrived French stranger Du Coudray.

"General Knox, who has deservedly acquired the character of one of the most valuable officers in the service," Washington wrote to Congress, "would consider himself injured by an appointment superseding his command." Knox, in fact, mailed Congress his resignation. Generals Nathanael Greene and John Sullivan sent Congress nasty notes threatening to quit. Congress got paranoid that the military leadership was attempting to undermine civilian authority and passed a resolution asking the generals to apologize. The lawmakers had as much hope of getting the offending officers to say they were sorry as the East India Company had of being reimbursed for its waterlogged tea. Because Du Coudray proclaimed to Congress that he was "the most learned officer in France" and an aristocrat "so near the throne," as John Adams put it, the delegates worried that offending Du Coudray was the equivalent of insulting Louis XVI, whose official help Benjamin Franklin was in France working to obtain.

Though the Du Coudray dilemma was one of the war's dumber deadlocks, a hapless Lafayette stumbled right into the middle of it. Luckily some new French engineers personally recruited by Franklin landed in Philadelphia, including the soon-to-be-invaluable future chief engineer of the Continental Army, Louis Duportail. The new arrivals set the Congress straight on the poser Du Coudray. Then Du Coudray was nice enough to drown when he and his horse fell in the Schuylkill River. Win-win: Knox happily kept his job, and the horse lived. As for the source of the aforementioned confusion, Silas Deane: his days were numbered.

As the culmination of the patriots' indignation about French officers, the Du Coudray business narrowed Lafayette's chances of being hired on. Still, the aristocratic Lafayette was also so close to the French monarchy he had stepped on Marie Antoinette's toes on the dance floor of Versailles. Those credentials stirred up the same congressional heebie-jeebies about insulting the French court as the Du Coudray incident had. For men who signed a document declaring that all men are created equal, the Continental Congress sure spent an awful lot of time kowtowing to French bigwigs.

A letter to the Congress signed by Franklin and Deane in Paris introduced Lafayette as "exceedingly beloved" and "a young nobleman of great family connexions here." Furthermore, "The civilities and respect, that may be shown him, will be serviceable to our affairs here, as pleasing not only to his powerful relations and to the court, but to the whole French nation." In other words, a failure to welcome this kid to Philadelphia would be seen as a faux pas in Paris and Versailles.

If his swanky backstory wasn't reason enough for the delegates to reverse their initial knee-jerk rejection, Lafayette delivered to Independence Hall a letter that would thaw the cold, cold hearts of needy patriots. "After the sacrifices I have made," he wrote, "I have the right to exact two favours: one is, to serve at my own expense,—the other is, to serve at first as a volunteer."

Compared with the demands of the previous boatloads of French opportunists, this was the generous offer of a good egg. It's worth noting that right from the start, America brought out the best in Lafayette, as if he had vomited up his adolescent petulance somewhere in the middle of the Atlantic and come ashore a new and wiser self. General Nathanael Greene later described Lafayette as "a most sweet tempered young gentleman."

On July 31 Congress commissioned him as a volunteer major general, which is to say, he was basically an unpaid intern wearing a general's sash. The resolution acknowledged that he had "at his own expence come over to offer his services to the United States without pension or particular allowance, and is anxious to risque his life in our cause."

Lafayette was able to hire as aides two of the men who had sailed with him, Louis de la Colombe and Jean-Joseph de Gimat. The others, except for Kalb, would eventually give up and go home. Congress would finally grant Kalb a commission as a major general in September, after he threatened to sue them for reneging on Silas Deane's contract. (Kalb then broke the news to Broglie that the Frenchman's scheme to replace Washington as commander in chief was "impossible to execute.")

A few days after Lafayette received his commission, Washington arrived to meet with Congress. The Howe brothers' fleet was spotted off the Jersey shore, a portent of trouble for Philadelphia.

Lafayette then met his new boss at dinner with some congressmen at City Tavern. If the menu of the present-day replica of the aforementioned eatery is any indication, I hope they were in the mood for sauerkraut.

They didn't call Washington "His Excellency" for nothing. Recording her initial sighting of the six-foot-four Virginian for her husband, Abigail Adams wrote, "I was struck with General Washington. You had prepared me to entertain a favorable opinion of him, but I thought the half was not told me." Sizing up his civilian allure along with his martial charisma, she noted, "The gentleman and soldier, look agreeably blended in him. Modesty marks every line and feature of his face."

As the starstruck Lafayette later described his first glimpse of Washington, "It was impossible to mistake for a moment his majestic figure and deportment; nor was he less distinguished by the noble affability of his manner." What a sweet memory. Still, it does get on my nerves how easy it is for tall people to make a good first impression.

Lafayette later recalled that Washington spoke to him "very kindly" and acknowledged the boy's "sacrifices . . . in favor of the American cause." Impelled by congressional urging to look after this important son of France, as well as Lafayette's standing as a brother Mason, Washington invited Lafayette to join him at headquarters and asked the boy to "consider himself at all times as one of his family." Washington was referring to his military family or aides-de-camp, the same way John Adams described the aide Alexander Hamilton as "one of General Washington's Family." So when Washington said "family," he meant "chummy minion." The orphaned Lafayette heard "son."

"I wish to serve near the person of General Washington," Lafayette wrote to John Hancock a few days later. At least until "such time as he may think proper to entrust me with a division of the Army." While Lafayette seemed to accept, for the moment, that he was an honorary officer without his own command, he had not given up on that particular dream. In fact, his letter to Congress promising to work for free included his hope "to serve at first as a volunteer," meaning just that: at first.

Washington found the whole thing awkward and confusing. Writing to a Virginia congressional delegate in August, he wondered, "If Congress meant, that this Rank should be unaccompanied by Command I wish it had been sufficiently explain'd to [Lafayette]. If on the other hand, it was intended to vest him with all powers of a Major General, why have I been led into a Contrary belief, and left in the dark with respect to my own Conduct towards him?"

Aside from this "great chaos" as Washington saw it, Lafayette grew on him right from the start. He invited Lafayette to join him to review the troops posted north of the city along the Delaware River. Lafayette observed, "About eleven thousand men, ill armed, and still worse clothed . . . many of them were almost naked. The best dressed wore hunting shirts, large gray linen shirts used in the Carolinas."

Well aware that his men were supposed to confront the redcoats whilst dressed to shoot raccoons, Washington confessed to Lafayette, "We must feel embarrassed to exhibit ourselves before an officer who has just quitted French troops."

To Washington's relief Lafayette replied, "It is to learn, and not to teach, that I come hither." Observing the Continentals' marching skills or lack thereof, Lafayette attempted to put a cheerful spin on the half-naked bunglers. He reckoned, "Virtue stood in place of science."

While British soldiers were well clad in proper professional uniforms, "uniform" would not be the best description of their civilian government back home. Parliament, the font of the dreaded tax laws that incited the revolution, was nevertheless rife with pro-American MPs like Charles James Fox, who took to dressing up in the colors buff and blue as an homage to the palette of George Washington's military uniform. And Edmund Burke, who, in a pensive if Anglocentric speech before the House of Commons, pleaded for peace and reconciliation with the "descendants of Englishmen." Identifying the rebellion as an inherently British demand for civil rights, he warned, "To prove that the Americans ought not to be free, we are obliged to depreciate the value of freedom itself."

Then there was the inner conflict of men like Britain's secretary at war, Lord William Barrington, who confirmed in a 1775 letter to his prime minister about ratcheting up troop strength in the colonies, "It is my duty and inclination to make that measure succeed to the utmost." However, he added, "My own opinion always has been and still is, that the Americans may be reduced by the fleet, but never can be by the army." Which is to say that he was on top of flinging more red-jacketed infantrymen at the colonies while privately pointing out that unless the patriot miscreants would be polite enough to line up along Boston Harbor within cannon range of the British Royal Navy, then the whole damn thing was doomed.

Circa 1777, the most meaningful rift was a muddled lack of consensus about basic strategy among the British leadership. Initially, the British command's big plan for the war that year was to end it. This involved forces under the command of General John "Gentleman Johnny" Burgoyne moving south from Canada while General Sir William Howe led men north from New York City. They were to converge along the Hudson River at Albany. Since the British already controlled Manhattan and Long Island, sewing up the Hudson would isolate troublesome New England from the other colonies, delivering a mortal blow to the revolution.

Howe, the commander in chief in America, requested fifteen thousand recruits to seal the deal. The point man in London, the secretary of state for America, Lord George Germain, denied this request. By April, Howe grumbled to Germain, "My hopes of terminating the war this year are vanished."

Howe was still smarting from the embarrassment of Trenton. Plus, he was concerned that Gentleman Johnny, a part-time playwright, would hog the spotlight if they pulled off the Albany job. So Howe got it in his head to capture the rebel capital of Philadelphia, leaving Burgoyne to fend for himself in upstate

WILLIAM HOWE

New York. For what could be more glorious than occupying the largest city in British North America, seat of the treasonous Continental Congress? Howe repeatedly alerted Germain to this significant change of plans. Still, Germain somehow failed to understand that Howe and his troops wouldn't finish conquering Philadelphia in time to swing north to assist Burgoyne.

In the summer of 1777, the only person more confused by Howe's evolving scheme than Germain was George Washington. Washington not only believed Howe would veer north toward the Hudson, he also worried that Howe's helping Burgoyne was a "good policy" for the enemy. With the Northern Department of the Continental Army, under the command of General Horatio Gates, perched in New York to deal with Burgoyne, Washington's forces would confront Howe—somewhere. It was only because Howe's fleet was spotted sailing south from New York City that Washington was convinced that Philadelphia might be the target. Even then, Washington couldn't quite believe it, writing, "I caught myself casting my eyes continually behind me." It did not calm Washington's nerves that Howe sailed right on past Delaware Bay, a logical entry point for an invasion of Pennsylvania, and disappeared at sea for a few strange weeks (prompting speculation of an attack on Charleston).

The reason the American commander was waiting around to react was that, in 1777, Washington's plan to outsmart and outlive the enemy was to try not to die. This was the so-called Fabian strategy, named for the Roman general Fabius Maximus, the Cunctator ("the delayer"), who spent years wearing down the deadlier Carthaginians by retreating every time his opponents seemed poised to prevail, thus holding the Roman army together; basically, Fabius annoyed his enemies to death.

After the fiasco of the New York campaign, Washington returned to the question he hollered amid the sloppy retreat from Kips Bay: "Are these the men with which I am to defend America?" The unfortunate answer—yep—prompted him to face the grim fact that "it is impossible, at least very unlikely, that any effectual opposition can be given to the British Army with the Troops we have." Hence the plan to play to his army's strengths. The men might have been lacking in skill and discipline, not to mention ammo and food, but given their behavior in New York, they were not inexperienced at running away.

In March, Washington sent General Nathanael Greene to break the news to Congress about this wise if not particularly stirring policy. The delegates immediately understood the implications for their home base of Philadelphia: while the army intended to take a stab at defending the city, perhaps it wouldn't be the worst idea for the delegates to start looking into office space out in York County? In the event of a full-scale British attack on the capital, the politicians should be prepared to join the soldiers in their mad dash to who knows where. From Philadelphia, John Adams attempted to convince Abigail, or perhaps himself, "We are under no more Apprehensions here than if the British Army was in the Crimea. Our Fabius will be slow, but sure."

Washington got word that Howe's missing fleet had finally popped up in Chesapeake Bay. On August 24, he led his scruffy army, including his new general, Lafayette, through the streets of Philadelphia. John Adams, observing the parade, lamented to Abigail, "Our soldiers have not yet, quite the Air of Soldiers." The not-quite-soldiers continued marching twenty-five miles or so southwest toward Brandywine Creek and Chadds Ford. On August 25, around thirteen thousand British forces landed in Maryland about sixty miles south of Philadelphia and advanced north toward the coming confrontation in the Brandywine Valley on September 11.

The place looks wrong. I'm not bothered that the present intrudes on the past, what with the combination Pizza Hut–Taco Bell looming near a road once crammed with redcoats; or that Fuzzy Butts Dog Daycare is situated a stone's throw from the old Quaker house where Lafayette reportedly spent the night before the battle. No, my problem is springtime. The Brandywine countryside is in bloom—too green, too chirpy, too full of life.

Alas, it's May. I guess somewhere in the back of my mind I was pining for the leafless trees and frozen earth in the paintings of the late local artist Andrew Wyeth. His pictures of this region summarize the soulful emptiness of a country where, as Gertrude Stein observed, "there is more space where nobody is than where anybody is." The occasional solitary figures in Wyeth's landscapes look like somebodies—a boy and his shadow running down a barren hill, a solemn woman watching over a snowy yard. When he painted Brandywine Battlefield in winter, it was a perfectly bleak clearing behind a pale man in a wool cap. Today the place smells like hope and freshly grown grass.

Brandywine Creek empties into the Christina River across the Delaware state line. That the river was named for a queen of Sweden and that its tributary may have been named after a Dutchman called Brantwyn hint at the area's older colonial past. It was New Sweden and then New Netherland prior to King Charles II signing it over to the Quaker William Penn in 1681. Long before Englishmen and a handful of Germans came to Penn's Woods and started putting up the stout stone houses Andrew Wyeth often rendered, the Swedes in these parts had introduced the log cabin to America. No wonder Wyeth often painted the place in egg tempera, the medium of the old Netherlandish masters—these wooded hills and planted fields have a decidedly northern atmosphere, as in northern Europe, which is curious considering Chadds Ford is less than twenty miles from the Mason-Dixon Line.

Elkanah Watson, an employee of the Rhode Island merchant and slave trader John Brown, traveled through the area on business during the revolution. After spending time farther south, he noted in his journal that he preferred Pennsylvania: "The verdure of the fields, and the neatness and superior tillage of the farms in the rich vales, were so grateful to the eye." Chalking up the difference to "but one cause," an absence of slavery, he wrote, "Here we witness the impulses and results of honest industry, where freemen labor for themselves." Watson did, however, note the bad roads.

Nick, my Philadelphia-based driver, and I think the roads around here aren't bad—just the confusing kind of picturesque. Unlike George Washington, I have a good map. To Nick, there is no such thing. Even though he must be ten or twenty years older than I am, he is entirely addicted to his dashboard GPS, and he sighs theatrically at the page I've ripped out of a Pennsylvania road atlas and marked up with the approximate locations of various landmarks and whatnot related to the Battle of Brandywine and/or Lafayette.

When Nick picked me up at my Philly hotel that morning, I told him that I wanted to start in Chester County at a monument to Lafayette erected by area schoolchildren. An astounding five thousand people attended its dedication on September 11, 1895.

Five thousand was not a number that interested Nick. He pointed at his GPS gadget and asked, "What's the address?"

I replied that I didn't think it had an address, that it was more like a skinny sculpture out in the country by the side of a road. I pointed at the town of Chadds Ford on my map, and suggested we head that way and just ask around once we get there. He said nothing, grabbed the map page, got out of the car, and disappeared into the hotel for twenty minutes like William Howe and his mystery fleet. Apparently he was in there trying to track down the address of a thing without an address, because he came back and barked, "No address!"

Starting to worry that this dillydallying was going to make me miss *A Son of Liberty*, the Lafayette-themed puppet show I planned on catching at the Battle of Brandywine reenactment that afternoon, I rifled around my papers and found an actual address for a cemetery named after Lafayette that I wanted to check out in West Chester. Nick punched the digits into his beloved contraption, and finally we were off down I-95 for a carefree day reliving one of the biggest, dumbest skirmishes of the revolution.

On September 11, 1777, about eleven thousand Americans confronted thirteen thousand or so Britons and Hessians within ten square miles of Brandywine Creek. Nowadays, this clash is remembered, if it's remembered, for its commanders' mistakes—the unfortunate long-term repercussions of Howe's victory and Washington's tactical blunders day-of. Which is one reason I was so keen on catching the afternoon's reenactment festivities promising "Battles! Music! 18th-century celebrities!" I was curious how area boosters would splice together a celebration out of this particular clip from the patriot blooper reel. Especially since one factor in Howe's overwhelming triumph was the superior intel he received from Loyalist valley residents, whom General Nathanael Greene, an ex-Quaker, ridiculed as "villinous Quakers . . . employed to serve the enemy."

When Howe and his troops crossed the Mason-Dixon Line and entered Pennsylvania on September 9, they passed, according to John Adams, "thro the very Regions of Passive obedience," meaning obedience to the king. Adams complained, "There is not such another Body of Quakers in all America, perhaps not in all the World." It should be noted that the Quakers could be excused for failing to dominate, say, Adams's home colony of Massachusetts, where in the previous century his Puritan ancestors were still hanging Friends on Boston Common.

Hessian officer Johann von Ewald noted in his journal that from some local Quakers they "received positive information here that the greater part of the American army had entrenched behind . . . the Brandywine."

Washington chose to make his stand at the Brandywine because it was the only significant topographical obstacle between present-day Elkton, Maryland, where the British landed, and their objective, Philadelphia. Officially a creek, the Brandywine was (and still is) often referred to as a river because of its river-y width, depth, and current. It was substantial enough to support a series of profitable mills up and down its banks—mostly gristmills and a few sawmills, along with the odd paper mill, including the one that produced the paper on which copies of the Declaration of Independence were printed.

As for Howe, he set up camp at the town of Kennett Square, and local Loyalists let him know that Washington had concentrated his forces about seven miles to the northeast near Chadds Ford, the creek's major crossing.

Washington was headquartered east of Chadds Ford in the stone house of mill owner Benjamin Ring, which still stands in Brandywine Battlefield Park. From there, he coordinated the Continental regulars and regional militias positioned along the eastern, Philadelphia side of the creek at what he assumed— incorrectly—were all the other traversable fords.

After the battle, Timothy **Pickering**, a colonel from Massachusetts, jotted down a few lessons the patriots learned too late. He noted "the importance of good maps of the country," the value of having "guides perfectly acquainted with every road," and the necessity of conducting proper recon. "Before the battle of Brandywine," he wrote, "we had time to have viewed all the ground several miles on our right, but did not do it."

At one of the patriots' northernmost defenses along the creek, Washington posted troops commanded by General John Sullivan, a New Hampshire attorney and delegate to the First Continental Congress. Sullivan and his men ended up, as Lafayette put it, "fated to receive all the heavy blows." A few weeks after the battle, Washington wrote to Sullivan, "We were led to believe, by those whom we had reason to think well acquainted with the Country, that no ford above our [pickets] could be passed, without making a very circuitous march."

Oops: Generals Howe and Cornwallis had nearly eight thousand men up at four o'clock on the morning of September 11 and trudging stealthily toward undefended northern crossings of the Brandywine that Washington was unaware of.

Meanwhile, by six o'clock that morning, a smaller column of about five thousand Brits and Hessians commanded by the Prussian baron General von Knyphausen were making haste to the Brandywine's western bank at Chadds Ford, where Washington expected them to show up—that being the point. Knyphausen's orders from Howe were to "amuse the Americans." By which he meant hoodwink the Continentals into believing they were holding their own against Howe's entire army while the bulk of it was en route to sneak up behind them. The morning fog, followed by smoke generated by artillery fire exchanged across the creek, not to mention the exasperating trees, abetted the misdirection, cloaking Knyphausen's troops and dooming any American attempt to get an accurate British head count.

According to the journal of the then captain of the Seventh Royal Fusiliers, John André, "The design, it seemed, was that General Knyphausen, taking Post at Chad's Ford, should begin early to cannonade the Enemy on the opposite side, thereby to take up his attention and make him presume an attack was then intended with the whole Army, whilst the other Column should be performing the *détour*."

The subtle hills that framed Andrew Wyeth's compositions were also pretty handy for concealing terrifying quantities of redcoats of the move.

After a dizzying morning of driving up and down the area's winding roads in search of battle landmarks, I play hooky for a bit to duck into the Brandywine River Museum, housed in a converted nineteenth-century gristmill along the east bank of the creek near the spot where Henry Knox's artillery corps was lobbing cannonballs at Knyphausen.

I can't pass up the chance to get a glimpse of the museum's collection of paintings by Wyeth as well as those of his father, son, and neighbors. Unaware of just how overwhelmed I have been by the crannies of this landscape, I hear myself exhale next to a painting by Andrew's father, N. C. Wyeth, of Sacagawea giving Lewis and Clark directions. She's standing on a ridge before a big Western landscape like the one I grew up in near the headwaters of the Missouri. I am suddenly smote with homesickness, partly because I miss Montana, but mostly because I pine for the clarity of altitude. Sacagawea looks like she can see for fifty miles in any direction, whereas the undulations and abundant tree clumps of the Brandywine Valley offer the outsider no such perspective.

Never getting the lay of the land around here was one of Washington's biggest problems. And not just Washington's—at one point a brigade of British grenadiers got lost in some woods and turned up in an entirely different location from where they had been ordered; luckily for them, there were plenty of rebel scum to shoot at where they ended up.

Washington received contradictory reports about Howe's intentions and whereabouts all day long. Every time the general heard rumors of redcoats moving north—including sightings of the sort of visible-from-space dust clouds thousands of boots were bound to kick up—he either waved off the reports or assumed they were the result of fake-outs masterminded by Howe to lure unsuspecting patriots into ambushes. Having spent the previous six months second-guessing Howe's plans, including much of the summer wondering where the hell the fleet was, Washington was suspicious of his opponent—just not suspicious enough. In keeping his guard up about Howe's sneakiness, Washington underestimated the scope of Howe's sneakiness.

That afternoon General Sullivan sent a message to the Ring house alerting Washington that Britain's main army had crossed the Brandywine's northern fords and turned south in a kind of buttonhook of doom. Sullivan fretted that British brigades were about to descend on his men.

This turn of events would have been worrisome for anyone, but for Sullivan and Washington the situation no doubt inspired a particularly humiliating feeling of déjà vu. They surely flashed back to the Battle of Long Island, when British and Hessian troops took Sullivan's troops by surprise because Washington had left a crucial pass into Brooklyn undefended.

Lafayette, who had celebrated his twentieth birthday five days earlier, had been hanging around headquarters all day. He begged Washington to let him go lend a hand to Sullivan. A flummoxed Washington failed to weigh the consequences of tossing such a precious symbol of France into a Pennsylvania meat grinder. So he gave the boy permission. Lafayette galloped off toward Sullivan along with his aides Gimat and La Colombe. Lafayette's concerns about finally taking his first crack at combat basically boiled down to *Danger! Yippee!*

Outfoxed, the Continental Army was cornered between Cornwallis and Howe's nearly eight-thousand-man force at the rear and Knyphausen's five thousand men at the front coming for them across the creek. Recalled one of the latter, "The water took us up to our breasts and was much stained with blood."

A series of cramped firefights that Sullivan described as "muzzle to muzzle" and grubby fits of man-to-man combat erupted up and down the eastern banks and across the surrounding hills and fields. A British captain who had been marching with Cornwallis since four that morning witnessed "the balls ploughing up the ground. The trees cracking over one's head.

The branches riven by the artillery. The leaves falling as in autumn by the grapeshot."

At five o'clock, Washington fired off an update to the president of the Congress, reporting, "At half after four O'Clock, the Enemy attacked Genl Sullivan at the Ford next above this and the Action has been very violent ever since. It still continues." He noted, "A very severe Cannonade has began here too," meaning near Chadds Ford, adding, "I suppose we shall have a very hot Evening."

Jacob Ritter was the son of German immigrants who volunteered for one of the Pennsylvania militias after a stirring patriotic sermon by his Lutheran minister. He later recalled of Brandywine, "Towards evening . . . our battalion was ordered to march forward to the charge. Our way was over the dead and dying, and I saw many bodies crushed to pieces beneath the wagons, and we were bespattered with blood."

Ritter was so appalled by the day's patriotic gore that he had an epiphany: "It was contrary to the Divine Will for a christian to fight." Therefore he refused to take a shot at "my fellow-creatures." Later, he joined the Society of Friends, becoming a minister. It says something about the ugliness of September 11, 1777, that this boy woke up a Lutheran and went to bed a Quaker.

Lafayette, a descendant of Christian warriors stretching back to the Crusades, cheerfully belly flopped into the bloodbath. When he caught up to Sullivan, he noticed that the general "had barely enough time to form a line in front of a thin wood," when suddenly "Lord Cornwallis's troops advanced in perfect order across the field, his first line firing cannons and muskets." Even though the rebels returned "a murderous barrage of musketfire," Sullivan's right and left flanks got spooked and started running away, allowing the redcoats to "concentrate all their fire on the center of our line." Oh, if only that was the last time in America that the extreme left and extreme right broke down and made a mess of things, leaving everyone in the center to suffer.

While Washington's Fabian strategy allowed for considered, tactical retreats to keep the army together, random rattled fleeing was not what he had in mind. "The confusion," Lafayette recalled, "became extreme." Frantically struggling to put the toothpaste back into the tube, he rode back and forth to block the runaways, shaking his sword. At one point he jumped off his horse to clutch at the limbs of evacuees to literally hold them in place. And he succeeded, sort of, for a bit. "Whilst endeavoring to rally them," he later wrote to his wife, "the English honoured me with a musket ball, which slightly wounded me in the leg." What with the noise and chaos, Lafayette couldn't be bothered to slow down. Eventually, his aide Gimat spotted blood leaking from his left boot and helped him back onto a horse.

It started getting dark. With patriot losses at more than two hundred killed, five hundred wounded, four hundred captured, and a few precious cannons left behind during the day's withdrawals, Washington pulled the Fabian plug so his leftovers could live to lose another day. Having shrewdly held back in reserve a couple of divisions commanded by General Greene, Washington called them into service to provide cover for the

WASHINGTON

army's relatively dignified retreat to the town of Chester, about thirteen miles to the east. An aide to Howe conceded that Greene and his men "fought very bravely." Months later the Fighting Quaker would brag, "I think both [Washington] and the public were as much indebted to me for saving the army from ruin as they ever have been to any one officer in the course of the war."

At midnight, Washington sent the president of Congress a message from Chester. "Sir," he wrote, "I am sorry to inform you, that in this day's engagement, we have been obliged to leave the enemy masters of the field." After enumerating a few of the recent calamities, he nevertheless reported, "I am happy to find the troops in good spirits; and I hope another time we shall compensate for the losses now sustained." He then added, "The Marquis La Fayette was wounded in the leg."

At Chester, Lafayette got his leg patched up. One of the men helping Gimat and La Colombe take care of him was the nineteen-year-old captain of a regiment of Virginia regulars, James Monroe, the future president who would invite Lafayette back to America in 1824. Another future president showed up and made arrangements for Lafayette to be transported to Philadelphia to recuperate. As Lafayette recalled years later, Washington ordered his surgeon, "Take care of him as if he were my son."

Howe would be criticized later for permitting Washington's retreat and not finishing off the patriots then and there. But after the day's four a.m. wake-up call and fourteen-mile hike, John André confided in his journal, "Night and the fatigue the soldiers had undergone prevented any pursuit." While around ninety redcoats died, nearly five hundred were wounded. The Brits commandeered Birmingham Friends Meetinghouse to use as a makeshift hospital.

During the battle, patriot forces firing at team Cornwallis had hunkered down behind the rugged rock wall separating the meetinghouse from a burying ground where a mass grave would be dug to lay to rest some of the day's American and British dead. Now called the Birmingham Lafayette Cemetery, its focal point is an ostentatious, eighteen-foot-high commemorative phallus engraved with a corny poem about "Lafayette, the brave."

Unleashing a killing spree on Quaker property is a bit of a faux pas, a little like moseying into a Hindu temple with a wad of raw hamburger and plugging in a George Foreman grill. The Birmingham Friends' response to the Lafayette shaft is a humble if passive-aggressive "peace garden" a few steps away, a small yard with a simple stone marker on the ground engraved with the words of conflicted hawk Dwight David Eisenhower. It reads, "Every gun that is made, every warship launched, every rocket fired signifies, in the final sense, a theft from those who hunger and are not fed, those who are cold and not clothed."

A Quaker in a straw hat is standing next to that quote, so I say hello and we start shooting the breeze about Eisenhower. I mention that Ike also said, "All wars are stupid and they can be started stupidly." I'm pretty sure the last time I made someone's face light up like that was when I told my New Deal Democrat grandfather that I got a point taken off an elementary school test for failing to capitalize the word "Republican."

Built in 1763, Birmingham Friends Meetinghouse is a stone building with the pitched roof and white shutters of a child's drawing of what everyone but Quakers would call a church.

Inside, the Friends congregate in a quaint white room filled with rows of sturdy wooden pews. Quaker worship often takes place in silence, though anyone moved to say something is welcome to.

Maybe it's because I'm a nonbeliever who used to work in radio, but the one Quaker meeting I had been to, at Arch Street Friends in Philadelphia, was like listening to a whole lot of room tone. I sat there for two hours and no one said a thing. Or rather I thought it had been two hours when in fact I lasted precisely fourteen minutes. Not because it was boring, but because it was the opposite of boring—tense, in fact. At one point I crossed my legs and the sound of denim on denim was so loud, my knees seemed to be plugged into some imaginary amp. Which did make me appreciate how growing up in this hushed Quaker atmosphere could make a person denounce war for purely acoustic reasons. If the noise of one antsy visitor squirming in her seat was that jarring, how evil must actual gunfire sound? In the meeting, I found myself wishing for something interesting to listen to that might also drown out the ambient sneezes, as well as something we could all look at to avoid the awkward eye contact. I left when I realized that sort of communal spiritual experience does exist. It's called the movies.

When Nancy Webster, one of the members of Birmingham Friends, invites me to sit down in one of the pews to chat, I ask about the Quakers' silent services. She describes them as "not so much the absence of talking as the presence of god." Interesting. Hers is a more poetic, more profound description than what I call it: room tone. But a synonym for "room tone" is in fact "presence," the sound of a room that audio engineers record for editing purposes. Every place on earth at any given moment has unique acoustics based on who and what is there. So actors, broadcasters, and musicians always have to stop and be still for a minute while a recording is made of what seems like emptiness but is actually the barely audible vibrations of life itself.

I am tempted to reveal to this perfect stranger I have known for less than two minutes that I will probably think of her and what she said about the presence of god every time I walk into a recording studio for the rest of my life. What I actually do is get on with the more prosaic business of broaching the subject of the "Fighting Quaker," Rhode Island's General Nathanael Greene.

Raised as a Friend, Greene was reprimanded as a youth by Quaker authorities for reading too many books about war. He said he was going to keep reading them. (Turns out I should have kept that anecdote in mind before stumbling into a den of Quakers and announcing my intention to write another war book.)

When Greene quit the faith, he really quit the faith, helping found a local militia, buying more war books from Henry Knox's bookstore in Boston, and going on to become one of

GREENE

Washington's most trusted generals in the Continental Army as well as a hero of the Battle of Brandywine.

"He left," Webster quips of Greene. "He's not our problem."

She does want to talk about the hardships suffered by the local people. The armies passing through outnumbered the residents, and both sides ransacked regional farms. A week before the Battle of Brandywine, Washington issued general orders "to prevent our own army from plundering our own friends and fellow citizens," asking, "Why did we assemble in arms? Was it not . . . to protect the property of our countrymen? And shall we to our eternal reproach, be the first to pillage and destroy?" It was a good point, but so was the complaint he sent to Congress a couple of months earlier. He griped, "With respect to Food, considering we are in such an extensive and abundant Country, no army was ever worse supplied than ours." Looting ensued.

"This area gets stripped after the harvest," Webster points out. "The army takes your animals, your wagons, what you harvested, even your seed. They just stripped everything. The British were here for five days after the battle, which gave them plenty of time to raid."

On September 12, Thomas Paine was already labeling Howe "the chief of plunderers."

Gideon Gilpin owned the house where Lafayette was supposedly quartered the night before the battle (though he was also said to have stayed with Washington in the Ring house instead). Gilpin went on to file a claim for the items the armies filched from his farm after the battle, including "10 milch cows, 1 yoke of oxen, 48 sheep, 28 swine, 12 tons of hay, 230 bushels of wheat, 50 pounds of bacon, 1 history book, 1 gun."

As Webster and I talk, more and more of her comrades—mostly smiling, graying gentlemen wearing suspenders—keep filing in to sit in the pews and join the conversation. I tell them that I'm researching a book on Lafayette and that I'm planning to catch the Battle of Brandywine reenactment down the road. Turns out that's why they all showed up today, to chat up war enthusiasts and make them feel bad. "It's an opportunity," Webster says, "to say that war is not the only solution."

One of the other Friends introduces himself as Christopher Densmore, a curator at Friends Historical Library at Swarthmore, the nearby Quaker college. He says, "We understand our history as war." It is pretty clear by the way he's looking at me that by "we," he means "you," i.e., we non-Quaker Americans. The other Friends nod their heads in vexed agreement. Densmore laments, "If you go to the history section of the Barnes and Noble, it's all war."

First of all, let's not forget about *Cod.* I checked, and the book subtitled *A Biography of the Fish That Changed the World* is in stock at the two nearby B&Ns in Exton and at the Concord Mall, and for good reason—it's one of the better cod bios in print.

I do not think that there can ever be enough books about anything; and I say that knowing that some of them are going to be about Pilates. The more knowledge, the better seems like a solid rule of thumb, even though I have watched enough science fiction films to accept that humanity's unchecked pursuit of learning will end with robots taking over the world.

While I have come to the Brandywine Valley to trace a soldier's steps, I don't think I see American history as war. I see it as a history of argument, a daily docket of estrangement and tiffs—big and grand like the Lincoln-Douglas debates, big and stupid like the impeachment of President Clinton, or small and civil like what is happening at this moment with these strangers in these pews.

When Densmore complains that all the books in the history section are devoted to war, I almost blurt out that if he finds that fact so repugnant, maybe he should get cracking on writing books about other things. But I don't say anything, because every now and then I hear the voice of my nice church lady mother insisting that I mind my manners. For once, I actually regret holding my tongue. If I hadn't, then perhaps Densmore would have told me about the book he wrote on the Seneca orator Red Jacket, along with countless scholarly articles with titles like "The Quaker Origin of the First Women's Rights Convention." Which I found out about when I looked him up later. From what I can tell, he's one of the leading Quaker intellectuals of our time.

Densmore's book on Red Jacket is itself an argument for more books. Saddled with the nickname "Cow Killer" by fellow Indians allied with the British during the Revolutionary War, Red Jacket supposedly boasted that the blood on his ax was that of an American patriot he had killed, when in fact it was cow's blood. After that he was derided as a coward. Densmore writes, "The stories of Red Jacket's cowardice came from Red Jacket's political rivals . . . It is possible that they are overdrawn. Even allowing for bias, however, it seems clear that Red Jacket was no warrior. His later positions of leadership among the Seneca and the Six Nations reflect his political and oratorical skills, not his military merit." This levelheaded accounting strikes me as rational and factual, but it also seems like a slightly Quaker point of view another author might not have. A Friend would see Red Jacket *pretending* to kill a human as superior to actually killing one, even though this folly, if it happened at all, defied the code of eighteenth-century manhood, native or otherwise.

Moreover, precisely because there are plenty of straight-dope versions of the Revolutionary War in print, I have room to let these Quakers get under my skin for a minute. Partly because they have a point about how American publishers, writers, and readers fetishize state-sponsored violence and partly because I went to art school. Just as Densmore's religious ethics seem to filter through his nonfiction, my background bubbles up into mine. Having studied art history, as opposed to political history, I tend to incorporate found objects into my books. Just as Pablo Picasso glued a fragment of furniture onto the canvas of *Still Life with Chair Caning*, I like to use whatever's lying around to paint pictures of the past—traditional pigment like archival documents but also the added texture of whatever bits and bobs I learn from looking out bus windows or chatting up the people I bump into on the road. So these Quakers are just chair caning to me—learned, judgmental chair caning.

The most convincing if dispiriting argument for me to augment the supposedly unnecessary embarrassment of war books is that adding another one to the pile ups the odds of my fellow citizens actually cracking one open. In 2009, the American Revolution Center surveyed one thousand U.S. adults on their knowledge of the Revolution. Among the findings: "Many more Americans remember that Michael Jackson sang 'Beat It' than know that the Bill of Rights is part of the Constitution." A bleak revelation, and yet "Beat It" did win the 1984 Grammy for Record of the Year, so the numskulls who took the test knew at least one fact about American history. Sixty percent of those surveyed correctly identified the number of children parented by reality TV personalities Jon and Kate Gosselin, but over a third did not know the century in which the American Revolution took place. More than half of them believed the American Civil War preceded the Revolutionary War (whenever that was). Based on these findings, the situation appears to be more demoralizing than Americans understanding our history as war. What if we don't understand our history at all?

My friend Wesley Stace, a novelist and singer-songwriter, married a woman who was raised Quaker. When I was telling him about Birmingham Friends and researching a war book among people who are miffed about the very idea of more war books, he took their side.

"That's not a bad point that the whole of history is seen through war," he said. "It's very Quaker. I like it. I condemn your book. Previously I liked it and now I condemn it."

He added, "Did I ever tell you about the time I went to a

Quaker wedding? People were slightly horrified when the mother of the bride said, 'Of course I love my daughter—and I'm *learning* to love her husband-to-be.' To me, that's Quaker-ism in a nutshell: 'I'm going to say the right thing now, but I'm also going to be a little more honest than the situation calls for.' Quakers are all about frankness and honesty."

Wes and his wife, Abbey, send their kids to the Quaker school in suburban Philadelphia that Abbey attended. A school whose American history courses, Abbey contends, "encouraged a lot of questioning." She recalls, "They taught an awful lot about underdogs, the Underground Railroad, how black people were being treated. We learned the technical aspects of wars—where armies were and what happened. But I remember my history teacher senior year challenged the entire class to find mistakes in the textbook. You don't just accept anything as truth. You challenge it."

"There is a tendency," Christopher Densmore tells me, "for sectarian groups to know their history." After months of en-counters with Americans who were hazy on Lafayette's identity, it is a treat to talk to people who not only know exactly who he was but also actually have a problem with him—and, by exten-sion, with me.

One of the Birmingham Friends, yet another old man in a straw hat, is nice enough to walk me out to the car and give directions to the next deplorable, militaristic attraction on my to-do list. About a half mile down the road from the meeting-house, the 1895 monument to Lafayette stands near the general vicinity of where it's believed he got shot. It is a slender, fifteen-foot-tall Corinthian column taking up a patch of grass next to an appealing old yellow house. Nick drives by it three times before I stop confusing it with a streetlamp. Its Quakerish modesty is apparently the point. According to a commemorative booklet published by its sponsor, the Chester County Historical Society, "This simple and graceful shaft, made of terra cotta, at small cost, is a silent protest against extravagance and show in monuments."

All the same, five thousand celebrants gathered on this back road in Nowhere, Pennsylvania, to dedicate the thing. Its base is engraved, "On the Rising Ground A Short Distance South of This Spot LAFAYETTE Was Wounded at the Battle of Brandywine, September 11th, 1777." Also chiseled are sentiments expressed by Lafayette when he revisited the area on his tour in 1825: "The honor of having mingled my blood with that of many other American soldiers, on the heights of the Brandywine, has been to me a source of pride and delight."

Pride I get. Delight seems a bit demented. My uncle the vet had a long diagonal scar across his back from his shoulder to his waist, thanks to a Japanese bayonet slicing into him when he peeked out of a foxhole in the Philippines. I don't recall him being particularly giddy about it, but who knows, those World War II guys always were tight-lipped.

As Lafayette described the wound in a letter to his wife, "[It] hurt my leg a little, but it is nothing, my sweetheart; the ball touched neither a bone nor a nerve." The night of, Lafayette was a good sport on the long, dark slog from the Brandywine Valley.

Toward the end of the march he was lucid and persnickety enough to command his fellow stragglers to re-form into proper disciplined lines for their entrance into Chester. When he was finally laid out on a dining table to have his wound dressed, some fellow officers walked in and he made a wisecrack about hoping no one would eat him for supper. As he recuperated, he quipped to Adrienne, "If a man wished to be wounded just for his own amusement, he should come and see my wound and have one just like it." This best of all possible injuries came to represent his grit, good humor, and disregard for personal safety. Washington noted afterward, "The Marquis is determined to be in the way of danger."

The verdant corner of the Brandywine Valley where he was wounded looks so upstanding and American dreamy, there would be no indication of the mayhem that went down here unless this Lafayette doodad marked the spot. Gilbert Cope, one of the speakers at the 1895 dedication, decreed, "Amidst the shifting scenes of the Revolution it fell to the lot of this fair landscape to be the arena of war, horrible war!"

Kathy Garrison, the yellow house's owner, walks across the grass to say hello. She's about my age, friendly, what a cop on a police procedural would call a citizen. We jabber over the noise of her teenage son Chris mowing their well-kept yard. We marvel at the depth of feeling for Lafayette that could have summoned such a crowd to the dedication of this dinky tribute on the edge of her lawn. A crowd that was the same size as the mob of bobby-soxers screaming for Frank Sinatra at his breakout show/riot in New York City on New Year's Eve 1942. In the historical society booklet, the turnout is chalked up to "a spontaneous outpouring of the people, prompted by sentiments of patriotism."

On the other side of Garrison's house is Sandy Hollow Heritage Park, site of the day's battle reenactment. On September 11, 1777, a division of Virginians commanded by the Scottish-born General Adam Stephen tried to fend off Cornwallis in this big, open green space neighboring some woods. To underline that fact, the organizers of the reenactment posted a sign that says, "Beneath you, a Soldier of Washington's Army Bled to Give YOU LIBERTY." True enough, but how many more bled here unnecessarily because Washington screwed up?

I needn't have worried about how the event planners could possibly turn a bummer like Brandywine into a celebration. If Americans can transform Memorial Day, technically a remembrance of all our war dead ever, into the official kickoff of summer, we can handle adapting one demoralizing battle into a wholesome, chipper get-together.

When the reenactors march out of their encampment to line up on opposite sides of the field of battle, I hear a woman tell her children, "We know how this ends!" By which I think she means the patriots' ultimate victory in 1783, not them leaving behind their ordnance and four hundred POWs when they hightailed it out of here in 1777.

The sponsors have promised "Music! Battles! 18th-century celebrities!" and they deliver. Parents hound a George Washington impersonator for cell phone photos of him with their children as if he were Mickey Mouse. The battle reenactment takes place behind a safety fence too far away for spectators to get any real sense of the chaos unleashed here in 1777, though that's probably what the inhabitants of such a litigious society deserve. At least the artillery is loud. I bump into Kathy Garrison during the cannon barrage and she frets, "My dog must be going nuts."

As for the "Music!" it is mostly "Fifes!"

Oddly enough, the most historically detailed presentation during the festivities is the Penn's Woods Puppet Theater's presentation of Lafayette's biography in puppetry form. Sitting on hay bales with the under-ten set, I am impressed with how many facts they cram in. The Lafayette puppet, who has a high-pitched Monsieur Bill sort of voice, steps on the Marie Antoinette puppet's feet on the dance floor at Versailles, listens to the Duke of Gloucester puppet talk smack about his brother George III, abandons his puppet wife, gets bitten by mosquitos in South Carolina, fights in the revolution, and becomes, according to the Washington puppet, "the son I never had." All pretty accurate except for when the Beast of Gévaudan puppet lip-synchs "If I Only Had a Brain" from *The Wizard of Oz*, which is a crowd-pleaser thanks to its absence of fifes.

My favorite thing about the Brandywine shindig is just ambling around the reenactors' canvas tent city, scrutinizing the hobbyists and their stuff. I eavesdrop on a couple of sweaty infantrymen dressed up in the red wool getup of Britain's Forty-third Regiment of Foot, discussing their spouses' indifference to living history. One asks, "Does your wife put up with this?" He says it in a tone that implies that his wife barely puts up with this. His buddy answers, "Sort of. She let me hang my Monmouth photos in the upstairs hallway." The way he emphasizes the word "upstairs" hints that he and his memorabilia have surrendered the sweet spot above the living room mantel and decamped upstairs like Washington retreated to Chester.

There are female reenactors here, including a handful in Continental uniforms, perhaps channeling Deborah Sampson, alias Robert Shurtliff, a woman who pretended to be a man and enlisted in the Fourth Massachusetts. But most of them engage in the girl jobs of the camp followers: those civilians, including mistresses and wives (Martha Washington among them), who traveled with both armies to perform support roles such as doing laundry. A wench in a linen dress barbecues a cake in a tin pot over an open fire. "As soon as lunch was done," she coughs, "we got started on dinner."

Downwind from the cake smoke, I come across a pair of Continentals in the slouchy hunting shirts Lafayette described the first time he accompanied Washington to review the troops. The Yanks stare down the pretend Highlanders of the Eighty-fourth Regiment of Foot, the elite British battalion of Scottish emigrants to Canada that served in New York and down South. They're decked out in smart uniforms and black bonnets bedazzled with tufts of bear fur.

Pointing at the Highlanders, I ask the patriots if they ever find themselves wishing their army could afford such handsome duds.

"No way," one replies. "Who wants to wear wool on a hot day like this?"

Bet he'll be eating those words come winter at Valley Forge—words being just about the only thing there will be to eat.

To me, the highlight of the event is watching a reenactor in a long striped dress sitting alone on a blanket, winding yarn. Absorbed in the task of wrapping strands of wool around her hand, she never looks up. Watching her is so mesmerizing and oddly sacred that it never occurs to me to interrupt her and ask her name or how she got into the yarn-winding reenactment biz, maybe because she isn't recreating; she is creating.

Even though she and the parking attendants are about the only people around here doing anything remotely useful, nobody seems to notice her or her wool. But what she's doing, completing a step in manufacturing her own textiles, is as integral to and emblematic of the revolution as what was done by any Minuteman with a musket. Years before the first shots were fired, women like her were quietly sticking it to their colonial overlords with their needles and pins.

Between the Stamp Act of 1765 and Lexington a decade later, one of the colonists' most widespread tools of resistance against arbitrary taxation without representation was boycotting British imports, particularly luxury items. While the melodrama of hucking crates of tea into Boston Harbor continues to inspire civic-minded hotheads to this day, it's worth remembering the hordes of stoic colonial women who simply swore off tea and steeped basil leaves in boiling water to make the same point. What's more valiant: littering from a wharf or years of doing chores and looking after children from dawn to dark without caffeine?

An outgrowth of the colonists' non-importation agreements that emerged every time Parliament dreamed up a deplored new levy, the Homespun Movement was an extensive effort by American women to abstain from purchasing fabrics imported from Britain, particularly the finer ones like silk. Instead, they spun their own cloth to sew their families' clothes. For instance, the Yale graduating class of 1765 announced it would celebrate its commencement ceremony "wholly dressed in the manufactures of our own country," which was a college-boy way of saying their moms and sisters most likely tailored their suits out of wool from the household sheep.

After the Intolerable Acts of 1774 inspired a renewed wave of boycotts, John Adams wrote to Abigail, "I hope the Ladies are every day diminishing their ornaments, and the Gentlemen too. Let us Eat Potatoes and drink Water. Let us wear Canvass, and undressed Sheepskins, rather than submit to the unrighteous and ignominious Domination that is prepared for Us."

When Benjamin Franklin became the American envoy in Paris, he received a letter from his daughter, Sally, in Philadelphia asking him to send her French linen, lace, and feathers. He teased her that the request "disgusted me as much as if you had put salt into my strawberries. The spinning, I see, is laid aside, and you are to be dressed for the ball!" Yet Sally, along with her cohorts in the Philadelphia Ladies Association, still managed to sew 2,200 shirts by hand, which they donated to the "almost naked" Continental Army soldiers pitied by Lafayette.

The movement culminated in the moral, political, and sartorial victory of the brown homespun wool suit George Washington wore to his first inauguration in 1789.

Thus, "homespun" took on a deeper, grander meaning beyond handwoven women's work. It came to signify an earthy, self-reliant, utterly American way of life.

Because of Enlightenment thinker Jean-Jacques Rousseau's influential ideas about the virtues of natural man, the French were particularly enamored with such folksy charms. To escape the glitz of the palace of Versailles, Marie Antoinette built a pastoral farm getaway, a place where she could unwind in her plain muslin dresses and milk a cow or two for fun.

Ben Franklin's mission was to secure France's formal commitment as an ally. To him, it wasn't enough for the French to hate the British. The old flirt wanted them to fall in love with Americans. To that end, he reinforced their idealized notions of his plainclothed, plainspoken countrymen. Even though Franklin's impressive "scientific amusements" included making the first map of the Gulf Stream, in Paris he always made a point of appearing in public in a frontiersman's marten fur cap, so as to personify the rustic soul of America. Soon Frenchwomen were sporting weird wigs "à la Franklin," imitating his signature backwoods hat. If he could inspire Europe's most fashionable ladies to wear varmint hair, maybe he had a shot at convincing their menfolk to lend him their navy.

FRANKLIN

That dead animal on Franklin's bald spot blanketed a wily brain. When the gloomy news arrived in France that General Howe had occupied Franklin's hometown of Philadelphia after trouncing Washington at Brandywine, Franklin famously brushed off a French acquaintance's pity: "You mistake the matter. Instead of Howe taking Philadelphia, Philadelphia has taken Howe." Which was some seriously sly double-talk. But in the end, Franklin was not wrong.

Philadelphia's significance was more emotional than strategic. Whereas he who controlled the Hudson could restrict the lower colonies' access to and communication with New England, he who ruled the capital was in charge of a few very nice buildings—including Independence Hall and Franklin's house. What better symbol of a bruised rebellion than stashing wounded patriot prisoners of war in the structure where the Declaration of Independence was signed? Captain John André moved into Franklin's home, ripping off books and musical instruments as well as a painting of the homeowner that got shipped to England and wasn't returned to the United States until 1906. "Our enemies," Franklin groused, "made a prisoner of my portrait."

John Adams agonized over the ramifications of forfeiting the city. A few days after Brandywine he recorded his mood in his diary: "gloomy, dark, melancholy, and dispiriting. When and where will the light spring up?" He wondered, "Is Philadelphia to be lost? If lost, is the Cause lost? No—the Cause is not lost—but it may be hurt."

Sam Adams gave his colleagues a pep talk about the importance of not bellyaching in public. He declared, "If we despond, public confidence is destroyed, the people will no longer yield their support to a hopeless contest and American liberty is no more."

The wounded Lafayette, who had fled the capital with Congressman Henry Laurens of South Carolina, sent his wife a script for what the "wife of an American officer" should tell naysayers about the fall of "the rampart of liberty." He instructed her to spread the word that the British occupied "a poor forlorn town, exposed on every side, whose harbor was already closed." ('Twas closed at the war's outset when area patriots, including Franklin, installed obstructions in the Delaware River to block the enemy fleet's water access to the city.)

As the patriots' greatest propagandist Thomas Paine spun it, before bolting from the city ahead of Howe's entrance, "It is not a field of a few acres of ground, but a cause, we are defending."

That fall, every grain of truth washed ashore in France upon a wave of lies. One was that Johnny Burgoyne had conquered Albany and ruled the Hudson. Another was that Lafayette was killed in action. As Adrienne wrote of her protective mother, "She found a way to conceal the rumors of his death from me by taking me far from Paris."

Finally a letter dated the day after Brandywine arrived from Pennsylvania in which Lafayette assumed he was gently breaking the news of his injury to his wife as opposed to refuting gossip about his demise. He wrote, "I must begin by telling you that I am perfectly well because I must end by telling you that we fought a difficult battle last night, and that we were not the strongest." After downplaying his wound, he whimpered, "I will have to stay in bed for a little while, which has left me in a bad mood." For Adrienne, bad mood was an improvement upon dead mood.

"When Paris heard rumors of the first battles in which Lafayette and his companions did honor to the name of Frenchmen, there was general approval," wrote his friend Ségur. "The very persons who had blamed him the most for his bold enterprise"—including Adrienne's father—"now applauded him. The court showed itself almost proud of him and all the young men envied him." He concluded, "Thus public opinion, turning more and more toward war, made it inevitable and inevitably dragged a government too weak to resist in the same direction."

From Philadelphia, Lafayette was taken to recuperate among the Moravians, a community of German-American Jesus freaks in the future steel town of Bethlehem. Members of an old Protestant sect that predated Martin Luther, the Moravians abhorred violence. The Pennsylvania branch nevertheless set up a hospital to care for the men wounded in a war they denounced.

"The good Moravian brothers bewailed my passion for war," Lafayette later remembered, "but, while listening to their sermons, I was making plans to set Europe and Asia aflame." In one of his screwball memos to government officials back home, he outlined how the French state should strike at Britain's other colonies in Canada, the Caribbean, and India to pull focus from the redcoat crusade against the Americans. Never mind that France, despite its behind-the-scenes monkey business with Beaumarchais, still had a peace treaty with Britain. Prime Minister Maurepas, perhaps unaccustomed to receiving unsolicited foreign-policy advice from twenty-year-old French soldiers on the lam, quipped that Lafayette would have the government "sell all the furniture at Versailles to underwrite the American cause."

On October 1, Lafayette mailed Adrienne a bubbly update about the progress of his apparently adorable wound. "The surgeons are astonished by the rate at which it heals," he cooed. "They are in ecstasy every time they dress it, and maintain that it is the most beautiful thing in the world."

Meanwhile, in less orgasmic corners of the war, Washington attacked the British encampment at Germantown. He planned to surprise and surround Howe's long line of nine thousand Britons and Hessians camped in the town seven miles north of Philadelphia and force them to surrender—like Trenton, only bigger. Such a beefy offensive wasn't in keeping with his low-key Fabian strategy but his orders for the operation allude to the wounded pride provoking the beast within: "Our dearest rights, our dearest friends, and our own lives, honor, and glory and even shame, urge us to fight."

Washington divided his eight thousand regulars and three thousand militiamen into fourths. Well before dawn on the morning of October 4, four columns were to quietly converge from four directions, arriving on Howe's doorstep at the same time.

Is it appropriate to call a battle plan romantic? Of course this scheme was way too fussy for these crumpled misfits to pull off. Of course Nathanael Greene's forces would get lost in the fog and show up late. Of course the redcoat pros, no slouches they, would spot the early birds and sound the alarm before the rest of the stragglers could hit their marks. Yet there is something hopeful and endearing about Washington's belief in these men. That he actually trusted them to break off in quarters, march in the dark, and come together at some precisely timed rendezvous was an act of intrepid, starry-eyed faith and fealty. That got dozens of them killed, but still.

Howe, caught off guard by the earliest shots and as fogged in as everyone else, at first failed to understand the magnitude of the attack. When the initial patriot onslaught stupefied some nearby foot soldiers, Howe let rip the veddy British reprimand, "For shame, Light Infantry, I never saw you retreat before, form! form!" Afterward, one of his officers remarked how "pleased" the troops were when shots started whizzing by Howe's head "after he had accused the battalion of having run away from a scouting party." Howe later admitted that it simply had not occurred to him that "the enemy would have dared approach after so recent defeat as that at Brandywine."

On the one hand, Continentals under General "Mad" Anthony Wayne and General Stephen fought hard. On the other hand, the fog, thickened with gun smoke, prevented them from realizing they were shooting at each other and not the British. The fact that Stephen was drunk did not help.

A few dozen infantrymen with Britain's Fortieth Regiment of Foot holed up in the unfortunately well-built Cliveden, the house of the judge Benjamin Chew. In retrospect, the patriots should have just steered clear of it. But Henry Knox ordered an aggressive cannonade that proved futile against the mansion's thick stone facade. Ensconced in their elegant makeshift citadel, the redcoats picked off scores of Continentals with muskets fired from the upstairs windows. A British officer who was inside the house recalled of his enemy, "To do them justice, they attacked with great intrepidity . . . several of them were killed with bayonets getting in at the windows and upon the steps, attempting to force their way in at the door."

When Cornwallis arrived from Philadelphia with reinforcements, the Continentals began their customary retreat, and once again Howe let them slip away. While less than a hundred Britons and Hessians were killed, in the chaos of the fog nearly five hundred were wounded. Washington marched away with a thousand fewer men—about one hundred and fifty killed, more than five hundred wounded, and nearly four hundred taken prisoner. He did politely return one captive to the British: Howe's dog.

Surveying the aftermath at the Chew house the following day, the Hessian Johann von Ewald "counted seventy-five dead Americans, some of whom lay stretched in the doorways, under the tables and chairs, and under the windows." He added, "The rooms of the house were riddled by cannonballs, and looked like a slaughter house because of the blood splattered around."

While Washington once again managed to pull out with most of his battered crew intact, Germantown wasn't quite the jubilant ego boost he had hoped for. Then he got sucker-punched by some theoretically good news from upstate New

York. On October 17, General Burgoyne and his six thousand British and Hessian troops surrendered to Washington's underling, General Horatio Gates, at Saratoga.

Gates's ranks had swollen with new recruits and rookie militiamen screaming for British blood after some of Burgoyne's native allies scalped an area redhead. Gentleman Johnny was simply outnumbered, a fact that would come back to haunt Howe, given his decision to conquer Philadelphia instead of backing up Burgoyne.

On October 22, after receiving the news of his colleague's downfall at Saratoga, a deflated Howe wrote to Secretary of State for America Germain requesting to "be relieved from this very painful service . . . I humbly request I may receive his Majesty's permission to resign the command." The request would be granted, and he would sail home the following May. Even though Howe accomplished his stated goal of capturing Philadelphia, the side effect of siphoning off thirteen thousand men who could have reversed the outcome of Saratoga forever dented his reputation. Eventually, Howe demanded a parliamentary investigation to clear his name, but he would never shake off the blame for Burgoyne's surrender. Ditto Germain, for sloppy management. The buff-and-blue-wearing MP Charles James Fox denounced the bureaucrat as "an ill-omened and inauspicious character . . . unfit to serve the Crown."

As for Washington, how could he not envy Gates? Saratoga was the turning point of the war, the most spectacular patriot victory to date. And when it went down, His Excellency was more than two hundred miles away, licking his wounds from his recent setbacks.

Worse yet, Washington complained to Gates, "I cannot but regret that a matter of such magnitude and so interesting to our General Operations, should have reached me by report only." In other words, Gates did not inform his commander in chief directly but instead first alerted the Congress. Washington heard the news secondhand, a snub that contributed to his growing suspicions that Gates was plotting to replace him.

All Washington had to do to rack up some glory was the minor matter of recapturing Philadelphia. Too bad winter was coming and he commanded battered personnel whose most obvious characteristic, as he had written to the Congress after Brandywine, was "the want of Shoes."

Tempted by Philadelphia, Washington was nevertheless wise enough to invite his most trusted generals to talk him out of revenge fantasies. Nathanael Greene sanely pointed out that any attempt to recapture the capital "will be attended with vast expence and the loss of many lives to no valuable purpose." In one of the most perceptive sentences written in an era lousy with perceptive sentences, Greene predicted that an inevitable defeat in Philadelphia would "expose the weakness of the militia to the enemy and not only them but to all europe who now consider them much more formidable than they really are."

Lafayette agreed with Greene, writing to Washington, "Europe has a great idea of our being able to raise when we please an immense army of militia." A defeat in Philadelphia might prove otherwise. After all, "The american interest has always been since the begining of this war to let the world believe that we are stronger than we can ever expect to be."

When Lafayette and Greene hinted that the patriots needed to keep putting on a show of strength for "Europe," what they really meant was France.

On December 4, a messenger arrived at Benjamin Franklin's house outside Paris with news of Saratoga. "General Burgoyne and his whole army are prisoners!" he announced. The American envoys sent a quick message to Vergennes crowing about the "total Reduction of the Force under General Burgoyne himself & his whole Army having surrendered themselves Prisoners." Coincidentally, Beaumarchais was hanging around Franklin's house when the messenger turned up. The playwright, whose recently unloaded weaponry, ammo, and gunpowder contributed to the Saratoga success, was in such a rush to spread the word in Paris and/or pounce on profiting from it that he got into a carriage accident and broke his arm.

King Louis XVI wrote to his cousin and co-conspirator in the Beaumarchais plot, King Charles III of Spain, "The destruction of the army of Burgoyne, and the very confined state in which Howe finds himself have totally changed the face of things. America is triumphant and England beaten." Two days after learning of Saratoga, Louis notified Franklin and the American delegation they were welcome to officially reapply for French aid.

Saratoga is remembered as the breakthrough that goaded Louis's government to go public and recognize the independence of the United States. And that remains true, as the king's letter to his Spanish counterpart portends. Yet a perusal of the correspondence exchanged by French ministers from late 1777 to early 1778 also reveals how captivated they were with Washington's mettle at Germantown.

On December 7, Vergennes received reflections on the state of patriot affairs from the French ambassador to Great Britain, Adrienne Lafayette's great-uncle Noailles. According to his sources in London, Washington's army was holding up. It was more experienced and, based on its eager offense at Germantown, not afraid "to attack, or defend itself." Noailles wrote that the American encampment outside Philadelphia blocked Howe's access to the continent's interior and hindered his ability to forage for supplies. Hemmed in at the capital, Howe's army would soon be dependent on the navy, "his only resource for subsisting in a position where he will soon be encircled on all sides." True enough—occupied Philadelphia is remembered as a Tory party town, but food became short and crucial supplies, including firewood, grew scarce.

On December 12, Vergennes wrote to the American commissioners regarding Germantown, "Nothing has struck me so much as General Washington's attacking and giving battle to General Howe's army. To bring troops raised within the year to this, promises everything."

On the occasion of Lafayette's return visit to Brandywine in 1824, his secretary Levasseur acknowledged, "This battlefield was not remembered for a victory." But given the fact that there would have been no Saratoga if Howe's thirteen thousand troops had not been otherwise occupied duking it out with

Washington's in Pennsylvania, Levasseur noticed that the memory of the Philadelphia campaign "is no less dear to Americans who recall with gratitude the blood that their fathers and the young Lafayette spilled." Levasseur concluded, "Happy is the country in which events are appreciated more for their influence on the destiny of the Fatherland than for the glamour of the moment!"

After Brandywine, the wounded Lafayette suffered as much from boredom as from the hole in his calf. Fortunately his religious fanatic hosts out in the Pennsylvania hinterlands were kind enough to provide entertainment to while away his convalescence. Unfortunately for the cooped-up twenty-year-old, their idea of fun was lending out books about the accomplishments of Protestant missionaries in Greenland.

On October 14, 1777, Lafayette wrote to Washington, "Give me leave, dear general, to speack to you about my own business with all the confidence of a son, of a friend." The business in question being Lafayette's desire to command his own division, to actually be a general, as opposed to just being called one. He offered the commander his "respect" and "affection," at a moment in time when Washington was a little lacking in both. "I'l conduct myself by your advices," he pledged, adding, "I want to do some thing by myself, and justify that love of glory which I left to be known to the world."

Four days later he had not heard back from Washington, so

he wrapped his bum leg in a blanket and quit Bethlehem to ride to HQ and plead his case in person.

In a letter to the president of the Congress dated November 1–3, Washington wrote from his camp in Whitemarsh, around fifteen miles north of Philadelphia, "I feel myself in delicate situation with respect to the Marquis Le Fayette. He is extremely solicitous of having a Command equal to his Rank." Previously opposed to this, Washington had softened, recommending, "It will be adviseable to gratify him in his wishes." Compared with the other French officers Washington had so often railed against, he reported that Lafayette "is sensible, discreet in his Manner, has made great proficiency in our Language and from the disposition he discovered at the Battle of Brandy Wine, possesses a large share of bravery and Military ardor."

While Lafayette's letters home to France reflect his occasional delusions of grandeur, on the ground in America he apparently made a point of reining in his flights of fancy, especially around authority figures like Washington. Otherwise the stoic commander never would have gone on record complimenting the boy as "sensible." Lafayette wrote to his father-in-law, "I am cautious not to talk too much, lest I should say some foolish thing, and still more cautious in my actions, lest I should do some foolish thing."

Meanwhile, Howe's forces were swatting at the patriot fortifications along the Delaware River to open up water access to Philadelphia. Washington dispatched General Greene across the river to southern New Jersey to see what Cornwallis was up to, and Greene took Lafayette along. Greene tasked Lafayette to take a few hundred riflemen and militiamen to get a head count of the redcoat camp at Gloucester. It was the boy's first command.

On November 25, Lafayette hobbled stealthily close to the British base, eyeballed its troop strength, identified a vulnerable pocket of about four hundred Hessians, went back and fetched his men, and led them in ambushing the unsuspecting Germans. The patriots pursued the fleeing Hessians until backup from Cornwallis arrived. Greene informed Washington, "The Marquis, with about four hundred militia and the rifle corps, attacked the enemy's picket last evening, killed about twenty and wounded as many more, and took about twenty prisoners." He added that they "drove the enemy about half a mile and kept the ground until dark." Greene echoed what Washington had already written of Lafayette: "The Marquis is determined to be in the way of danger."

Careful not to exaggerate the incident's importance and to give his troops the credit, Lafayette wrote to Washington, "I want to acquaint your excellency of a little event of last evening, which tho' not very considerable in itself will certainly please you on account of the bravery and alacrity a small part of ours showed in that occasion." Regarding Greene, Lafayette, like a linebacker imploring his coach to put him in, declared, "I should have been very glad if circumstances had permitted me to be useful to him upon a greater scale."

Washington alerted Congress of Lafayette's modest success: "I am convinced he possesses a large share of that military ardor which generally characterizes the nobility of his country. He went to Jersey with Genl. Greene, and I find that he has not been inactive there."

Taking Washington's advice, Congress resolved, "That General Washington be informed, it is highly agreeable to Congress that the Marquis de La Fayette be appointed to the command of a division in the Continental Army."

Three days later, Washington put Lafayette in charge of General Stephens's division of Virginians—Stephens having been relieved of command after a court-martial found him guilty of drunkenness during the friendly fire incident at Germantown.

Lafayette celebrated his dream coming true by writing the biggest critic of his half-baked flight from France, his father-in-law, Jean de Noailles, the Duc d'Ayen. Lafayette informed the duke, "I have passed the whole summer without obtaining a division, which you know I have always wished for, and I have lived all that time at General Washington's house, where I feel as if I were a friend of twenty years' standing. Since my return from Jersey, he has offered me the choice, among several brigades, of the division I prefer, and I have selected one composed entirely of Virginians. It is weak in point of numbers at present, even in proportion to the weakness of the whole army; it is almost naked, though I have been promised cloth out of which I shall make clothes, and recruits out of which soldiers must be made in about the same length of time."

That Lafayette chose to command men from Washington's home state speaks to his affection for His Excellency. That his Virginians were in such a sorry state speaks to the army's general disarray in late 1777, as well as to that specific division's torments after some of them were mowed down by friendlies at Germantown.

Lafayette swooned to Noailles about Washington, "His name will be revered in every age, by all true lovers of liberty and humanity." After more than two centuries of hyperbole about ye olde Father of Our Country, Lafayette's hero worship sounds so trite, it seems hardly worth mentioning. I am, for instance, thinking of that time in 1842 when Abraham Lincoln, ignoring slackers like the Buddha and Jesus Christ, proclaimed, "Washington is the mightiest name of earth."

In autumn 1777, however, Washington wasn't even the mightiest name in the Philly suburbs. Young Lafayette's unbending faith that Washington would go down in history as a cherished icon was not the consensus among his fellow officers or their civilian overseers.

Even Washington's supporters in Congress couldn't help resenting him for their hundred-mile exodus across the Susquehanna to the village of York, their modest, improvised new capital.

On October 16, Congressman Henry Laurens contacted his son John, a member of Washington's military family and a friend of Lafayette's, complaining of "difficulty in the hall of Congress. There is a constant buzzing and confusion . . . among the delegates." Laurens lamented, "The general opinion is that the difficulty arises from the want of discipline in the American army."

Thanks to the sluggish pace of transatlantic communication, it would be months before the powers that be in America found out that the powers that be in France were less concerned about the wipeout at Germantown than dazzled with Washington's nerve at attempting it. Knowing that fact sooner might have soothed a few flustered rebels stateside, and maybe boosted patriot morale in that specific, eccentric way that only French accolades can. Like how it must quiet the mind of Bruce Willis that even though his fellow Americans never nominated him for an Oscar, the French awarded him the Légion d'Honneur.

When Lafayette's father-in-law, brigadier general of the armies of the French king, received his son-in-law's letter with the quip about having to whip a division of Virginians into shape in the amount of time it would take to sew a uniform, the old soldier must have shook his head in wonder, understanding Lafayette's awe of Washington for holding together his gaggle of amateurs.

The following spring, John Adams would arrive in France to replace recalled envoy Silas Deane. Adams wrote home to one of the Continental Congress delegates regarding what he had learned about French reactions to Washington's flop at Germantown versus Gates's star turn at Saratoga: "General Gates was the ablest negotiator you had in Europe; and, next to him, General Washington's attack on the enemy at Germantown. I do not know, indeed, whether this last affair had not more influence upon the European mind than that of Saratoga. Although the attempt was unsuccessful, the military gentlemen in Europe considered it as the most decisive proof that America would finally succeed."

Of course, that realization came later, well into 1778. In the meantime, circa autumn of 1777, Adams was still representing Massachusetts in the Continental Congress. And he was one of the riled-up patriot bigwigs toying with replacing Washington, the loser of Philadelphia, with the hero of Saratoga, General Gates.

The physician and former congressman Benjamin Rush, a signer of the Declaration of Independence, volunteered as a doctor during the Philadelphia campaign and wrote to John Adams in York a series of letters after Brandywine and Germantown deploring the chaotic state of Washington's troops. Describing Washington as "outgenerald and twice beated," Rush informed Adams, "I have heard several officers who have served under General Gates compare his army to a well regulated family. The same gentlemen have compared Gen'l Washington's imitation of an army to an unformed mob."

Rush has been identified as the author of an anonymous letter to Patrick Henry in Virginia, claiming, "The northern army"—the troops General Gates led to victory at Saratoga—"has shown us what Americans are capable of doing with a GENERAL at their head." It went on to assert, "The spirit of the southern army"—Washington's bedraggled losers in Pennsylvania—"is in no ways inferior to the spirit of the northern." The anonymous Rush suggested replacing the homegrown Washington with one of his British-born underlings like Gates or Charles Lee, or perhaps General Thomas Conway, a Frenchman of Irish descent recruited by Silas Deane (whom Lafayette had commended for his "brilliant" soldiering at Brandywine before he soured on him, labeling Conway more Irish than French). Rush believed that if one of those three took Washington's place as commander in chief, the southern army "would in a few weeks" be whipped into "an irresistible body of men."

Henry forwarded the letter to his fellow Virginian Washington, who reportedly recognized Rush's doctor-style handwriting.

Here we have arrived at the largely forgotten and ultimately unsuccessful conspiracy among a few congressmen and Continental officers to oust Washington that is referred to as the "Conway cabal." It is hazily understood because some of the conspirators covered their tracks later on, after George Washington became George Washington. Rush, for instance, convinced at least two of Washington's nineteenth-century biographers to edit him out of the episode. In 1895 the *Atlantic Monthly* even published Rush's 1777 letters to Adams as news.

What happened was, the opportunistic Conway went over Washington's head, writing to Congress requesting a promotion. When Washington found out, he wrote to Virginia delegate Richard Henry Lee, "General Conway's merit, then, as an Officer, and his importance to this Army, exist more in his own imagination than in reality." Knowing that Conway and Gates were angling for his job, Washington also threatened the congressman, saying, "It will be impossible for me to be of any further service, if such insuperable difficulties are thrown in my way."

The situation just got pettier from there. Conway wrote to General Gates about Washington, "Heaven has been determined to save your Country; or a weak General and bad Coun-cellors would have ruined it." Washington got wind of the "weak general" snub when an aide of Gates's let it slip to the underling of one of Washington's officers, who reported it to His Excellency. Washington wrote to Conway to complain. Conway backpedaled, reassuring Washington that the rumor was false, adding that instead of a weak general, Conway really thought of Washington as a "brave man." Then Conway wrote to Congress to resign, and the delegates not only refused his resignation but also gave him a promotion, dubbing him in-spector general of the Continental Army, a post requiring him to report directly to Congress, not Washington. So the dele-gates usurped Washington's command to promote one of his rivals and then assigned the backstabber to be Washington's au-ditor and congressional tattletale.

Lafayette characterized Conway as "an ambitious and dan-gerous man." Regarding the behind-the-scenes patriot soap opera, he confided to Washington, "Such disputes, if known by the enemy, would be attended with the worst consequences."

Lafayette's adamant defense of Washington during a tough time deepened and cemented their bond. He wrote to Wash-ington of his "most tender and Respectful friendship" and con-fessed, the "Sentiments of my Heart [are] much Stronger than a So new acquaintance Seems to admit. But an other Reason to be Concerned in the present Circumstances is my Ardent, and perhaps enthusiastic wishes for the Happiness and liberty of this Country." In other words, after only five months' acquain-tance, to Lafayette, Washington and America were one and the same. "I am now fixed to your fate," he added, begging Washington's pardon if "youth and friendship make perhaps myself too warm."

In his reply to Lafayette, Washington expressed "sentiments of the purest affection." Which is about as gushy as a George Washington interoffice memo gets. He added, "It will ever constitute part of my happiness to know that I stand well in your opinion." Regarding the "dirty Arts and low intrigues" of Conway, Gates, and their accomplices among the politicians, Washington, echoing *The American Crisis* by Paine, acknowledged, "We must not in so great a contest, expect to meet with nothing but Sun shine." He closed the letter predicting a victorious future sleepover at Mount Vernon: "My Dear Marquis, if you will give me your Company in Virginia, we will laugh at our past difficulties and the folly of others."

In the meantime, some of Washington's so-called founding brothers continued to consider dispensing with the leader later anointed "the indispensable man."

On October 26, John Adams, the very delegate who nominated Washington to be commander in chief back in '75, wrote to Abigail from exile in York about the bright side of Washington's recent washouts at Brandywine and Germantown. "Now We can allow a certain Citizen to be wise, virtuous, and good, without thinking him a Deity or a savior."

Adams implied that Congress called for an official day of thanksgiving partly to celebrate the victory at Saratoga and partly to rejoice that Washington had nothing to do with it. "Congress will appoint a Thanksgiving," he dished, "and one

Cause of it ought to be that the Glory of turning the Tide of Arms, is not immediately due to the Commander in Chief."

Then, cramming about two millennia of republican fears about hotshot warriors run amok into one offhand remark, Adams added that if Washington had been able to take credit for the collective glee over Saratoga, "Idolatry, and Adulation would have been unbounded, so excessive as to endanger our Liberties."

Adams's hero was Cicero, not Caesar. "All the ages of the world have not produced a greater statesman and philosopher," Adams wrote of the ancient thinker and politician who had a bone to pick with Julius Caesar for parlaying his military accomplishments into a new gig as dictator, the beginning of the end of Rome as republic. It was the same ongoing apprehension Senator Henry Clay would express a half century later about what he saw as the danger of electing "a military chieftain" like General Andrew Jackson in 1824. A Jackson presidency, Clay feared, would "guaranty that this republic will march in the fatal road which has conducted every other republic to ruin."

John Adams's fretting that too much adulation for George Washington could tempt the commander to thumb his nose at the Congress was healthy and shrewd if unwarranted. Washington turned out to be as staunch a republican as Adams was, believing in civilian control of the military to the extent that later in the war the general stopped disgruntled Continental Army mutineers at gunpoint from marching on Congress to demand back pay. And yet Adams's note to Abigail does read like a pencil sketch for that creepy painting in the Louvre of Napoleon crowning himself emperor.

In a letter to an old crony from the Virginia House of Burgesses, General Washington marveled at "the jealousy which Congress unhappily entertain of the Army." Deeming this envy distressing and unfounded, he traced it to "the common, received opinion . . . that Standing Armies are dangerous to a state." While pointing out that he understood such an attitude in peacetime, Washington avowed that in the middle of a war, "We should all be considered, Congress—Army &c., as one people, embarked in one cause."

In York, Congress convened in an unassuming country courthouse by day and piled into cramped, shared living quarters at night. Some delegates were taken in by townspeople, including a few local preachers. The Virginian Richard Henry Lee split a rental with Sam and John Adams.

In the ample inventory of kudos racked up by the two Adamses of Massachusetts, I can't imagine "world's greatest roommate" made the list. It's possible that over the course of the revolution, the greatest threat to the stability of the Continental Congress wasn't the rift about the morality of slavery but rather the long and grating nights the delegates spent in York, hearing each other snore.

As Charles Carroll of Maryland described the mood there, "The Congress does worse than ever, we murder time, and chat it away in idle, impertinent talk." That does sound congressional. At the very moment their revolution seemed to be going to hell, the founders floundered—they wavered, they gossiped, they played pin the tail on the scapegoat.

Some of the crankier delegates started lashing out at the man they blamed for their uncomfortable circumstances in York. Not General Sir William Howe, rumored to be cozily shacked up in occupied Philadelphia with a Loyalist's wife nicknamed "Billy Howe's Cleopatra." The congressmen instead passed the time grumbling about the neo-Fabius George Washington instead.

"Our affairs are Fabiused into a very disagreeable posture," carped Congressman Lovell, the gentleman from Massachusetts who months earlier had chewed out the newly arrived Lafayette.

Embarrassed that the patriot capital had fallen, some representatives were livid that Washington seemed to be doing precisely zilch to get it back. Sam Adams wrote to a friend, "If we do not beat [the British] this Fall will not the faithful Historian record it as our own Fault?" (If historian-adjacent, narrative nonfiction wise guys are allowed to weigh in, I will go on record as being cool with it.)

Lafayette bemoaned to Washington of "oppen dissentions in Congress, parties who Hate one an other as much as the Common ennemy." He went on to denounce the delegates as "stupid men" who "believe that attaking is the only thing Necessary to Conquer."

One reason some of the antsier patriots were egging on Washington to carry out some splashy Christmastime derring-do is that he had done exactly that the year before when he crossed the Delaware River to ambush a smattering of Hessians sleeping off their holiday cheer in Trenton. As General Nathanael Greene sized up the Trenton victory and a follow-up feat in Princeton: "The successes of last winter were brilliant and attended with the most happy consequences in changing the complexion of the times." However, he added, "I fancy it would be found we were no great gainers by those operations."

Thus Trenton accomplished nothing much more than tidings of empty comfort and hollow joy—things, it should be said, that in the fall of 1777 a lot of Americans were really in the mood for. But whereas Trenton had been lightly guarded by a thousand or so Hessian hired guns, occupied Philadelphia was being protected by ten times that number of British regulars who had just licked George Washington more than once. As Henry Knox summed up the situation in a memo to Washington about why a winter campaign to take back the city was such a bad idea, there was "the improbability & impracticability of surprising 10,000 veteran troops in a well fortified city."

Moreover, at least a third of the patriot soldiers were shoeless—and one of the top two components of boots on the ground is the aforementioned boots. Not that they were exactly bundled up above the knees either. Knox made note of the Continentals' "entire want of Cloathing to keep the men from Perishing from the cold Winter's Season." With temperatures dropping, how could men without shirts expect to fend off opponents so blatantly well equipped with outerwear that they were nicknamed the red*coats*?

Knox concluded his advice to Washington: "My Opinion is for putting the Army in good Winter Quarters: to repair the damages done: to recruit & reform the Army."

Congress begrudgingly agreed to that plan after a congressional fact-finding committee visited Washington's camp at Whitemarsh in early December and observed the army's desperation firsthand. One look at the barefoot wretches whose unclad torsos were shouldering the burden of the revolution and the congressmen unbuckled their own shoes, handed them to some shivering infantrymen, and pledged to trudge back to stupid old York and turn the Continental Congress into the world's most vindictive, productive shoemaking bee. If only.

All the congressional inspectors actually did was send Washington a snippy note blaming him for low morale. Penned on December 10, 1777, the committee's letter to Washington charged, "Among the many reasons offered against a Winters Campaigne we were sorry to observe one of the most prevalent was a general discontent in the army and especially among the Officers."

The congressional committee instructed Washington to hunker down in winter quarters so "that a reform may take place in the army, and proper discipline be introduced."

On that point, Washington and his officers agreed. Lafayette reassured His Excellency, "There we schall be quiete, there we can discipline and instruct our troops."

Valley Forge, here they come. About twenty miles northwest of Philadelphia, the new camp featured the natural defensive barriers of the Schuylkill River and its tributary Valley Creek, plus high ground in the form of a pair of hills, Mount Misery and Mount Joy. It was close enough to the occupied capital to deter Howe's forces from pillaging the countryside with abandon but far enough away from the enemy to regroup in peace, or at least to see them coming. Not that that would be an issue. The Brits would be too busy playing cards at City Tavern to bother slogging through the snow to harass Camp Crummy. The patriots' more daunting enemies, however, were happy to make the trip; influenza, dysentery, typhus, and typhoid were more industrious winter soldiers than the ones answering to William Howe.

On December 19, Washington led his men there. One of them, seventeen-year-old Private Joseph Plumb Martin, had scrounged up a scrap of rawhide and sewed himself a pair of moccasins, "which kept my feet (while they lasted) from the frozen ground." Though his homemade footwear chafed his ankles, he wrote, "the only alternative I had, was to endure this inconvenience or to go barefoot, as hundreds of my companions had to, till they might be tracked by their blood upon the rough frozen ground."

An indignant Washington wrote to a friend of witnessing "men without Cloathes to cover their nakedness—without Blankets to lay on—without Shoes, by which their Marches might be traced by the Blood from their feet."

If it seems like it couldn't have gotten much worse than the iconic Valley Forge visual of bloody footprints in the snow, according to Lafayette, it was: "The soldiers lived in misery; they lacked for clothes, hats, shirts, shoes; their legs and feet black from frostbite—we often had to amputate." Bloody feet were preferable to no feet.

Congressman Henry Laurens, a Washington sympathizer, wrote to a friend back home in South Carolina, "General Washington complains of the want of many essential articles for the army. He is the most to be pitied of any man I know."

Private Martin reported, "We arrived at the Valley Forge in the evening; it was dark; there was no water to be found, and I was perishing with thirst." Failing to find any food or water, he confessed, "I felt at that instant as if I would have taken victuals or drink from the best friend I had on earth by force." Spotting some fellow soldiers pass by his tent with canteens full of water, he asked for some, and they refused. He asked for directions to the water, but they were too disoriented in the darkness to point the way. Finally, Martin paid them his last three pence for a sip.

In a message published in the March 1950 issue of *Boys' Life* magazine, Governor James H. Duff of Pennsylvania welcomed the forty thousand Boy Scouts who would be pitching their tents at Valley Forge at the upcoming National Boy Scout Jamboree, claiming the boys would "take away from Valley Forge a greater understanding of what makes America the greatest nation in the world today."

The scouts who convened at Valley Forge spent the Fourth of July with General Dwight Eisenhower. George Washington, Ike told them, "seemed deserted by the Continental Congress . . . He lost, from starvation and freezing, during that winter, more than three thousand"—it was actually closer to two thousand—"out of his tiny army." Washington's task—his "burden," Eisenhower called it—was "hearing the pitiful cries of the suffering and witnessing the despair in the eyes of the dying."

If anyone personified "what makes America the greatest nation in the world today" five years after V-E Day, it was Eisenhower. And he tried, for a moment, to hint at the truth: that what happened during that winter at Valley Forge was an embarrassment, a monstrous administrative and humanitarian fiasco, a self-inflicted wound.

When Lafayette wrote his letter to Washington worrying that America could lose the war not at the hands of the redcoats but rather "by herself and her own sons," he might not have been referring solely to the Conway cabal. He may have also had in mind the observable fact that the military, congressional, and state bureaucracies responsible for supplying the common soldiers with luxuries like food, water, and shoes were, to use an acronym coined by the grunts of Ike's war, FUBAR.

Any elected officials tempted to crow about how Valley Forge teaches the lesson of "what makes America the greatest nation in the world" would do well to page through E. Wayne Carp's sobering study of the administrative history of the Revolutionary War, *To Starve the Army at Pleasure*, a three-hundred-page summary of the biblical proportions of the plagues of locusts and darkness unleashed by the American powers that be on the patriot foot soldier.

"Historians agree," notes Carp, "that the major cause of the dearth of food at Valley Forge was not its scarcity—crops were abundant that year—but the lack of wagons to transport it to camp." And even if there had been enough wagons, there were not enough drivers. "The duty," Nathanael Greene wrote of the thankless hardship of traversing bad roads in bad weather, "is disagreeable in itself."

Turf wars among Congress and state and local authorities contributed to the chaos. Carp notes, for instance, that a shipment addressed to General Washington of much-needed "clothing earmarked for Continental troops was discovered stored at Fishkill," and the Fishkill Committee of Safety swiped it for New York recruits to wear.

These and other administrative challenges were made worse at Valley Forge because Quartermaster General Thomas Mifflin, the head of the supply corps, resigned his post in October 1777, two months before the army moved there. Mifflin, a Pennsylvanian, quit in a huff because Washington let his hometown of Philadelphia fall to the British. "Though General Washington repeatedly urged Congress to appoint a successor," writes Carp, "it did not fill the post until 2 March, 1778. The delay of nearly five months"—coinciding with winter at Valley Forge—"almost proved fatal to the Army."

When I visited Jefferson's Monticello, I took a tour of Mulberry Row, the plantation's slave quarters. The guide listed the weekly food rations for an adult male slave—two gallons of cornmeal, a half pound of pork or beef, four to five salted fish, a bit of molasses—making the point that it wasn't enough to live on, hence the slaves' need for personal vegetable gardens to supplement their caloric intake just to survive. Seemed like half the people on my tour shook their heads about what a shame it was to have to spend all day out in the fields only to trudge home to do more gardening—and it was. But I couldn't help wondering if the grunts at Valley Forge, with their chronically empty stomachs, would have envied Jefferson's half-full slaves.

There is a saying about supply lines attributed to both Frederick the Great and Napoleon Bonaparte: "An army marches on its stomach." My money's on Napoleon, if only because after he invaded Russia, his cavalry had to shoot its horses to eat as food.

In 1777, the Continental Army was two years old. The officers and politicians supplying the soldiery were no more experienced at getting blankets to the troops than the troops were at standing in a line and fending off Cornwallis and his veteran regulars, fighters well clothed and well fed through an efficient supply system whose kinks had been worked out over generations. And just as the troops at Valley Forge were about to undergo a serious program of self-improvement, so would patriot logistics. Not that this progress was going to bring back to life the two thousand corpses who would never march out of there come summer.

I would like to see the calamity at Valley Forge as just the growing pains of a new nation. It has been a long time since the men and women serving in the armed forces of the world's only superpower went naked because some crooked townies in upstate New York filched their uniforms. But there's still this combination of governmental ineptitude, shortsightedness, stinginess, corruption, and neglect that affected the Continentals before, during, and after Valley Forge that twenty-first-century Americans are not entirely unfamiliar with.

While I was reading *To Starve the Army at Pleasure*, the Veterans Affairs secretary was forced to resign after the revelation of widespread mismanagement of VA hospitals, including, CNN reported, "at least 40 U.S. veterans [who] died waiting for appointments at the Phoenix Veterans Affairs Health Care system, many of whom were placed on a secret waiting list."

I'm not just thinking of the Pentagon's blunders, though. I'm thinking of how the noun "infrastructure" never appears in an American newspaper anymore without being preceded by the adjective "crumbling." Or how my friend Katherine, a public high school English teacher, has had to pay out of her own pocket for her classroom's pens, paper, paper clips, thumbtacks, and, she says, "chalk when I run out," chalk being the one thing her school system promises to provide its teachers for free.

It's possible that the origin of what kept our forefathers from feeding the troops at Valley Forge is the same flaw that keeps the federal government from making sure a vet with renal failure can get a checkup, and that impedes my teacher friend's local government from keeping her in chalk, and that causes a decrepit, ninety-three-year-old exploding water main to spit eight million gallons of water down Sunset Boulevard during one of the worst droughts in California history. Is it just me, or does this foible hark back to the root of the revolution itself? Which is to say, a hypersensitivity about taxes—and honest disagreements over how they're levied, how they're calculated, how that money is spent, and by whom. The fact that the Continental Congress was not empowered to levy taxes was the literal reason for the ever-empty patriot coffers. More money would have helped, but it wouldn't have entirely solved the problems of a loosely cinched bundle of states trying to collaborate for the greater good.

Whatever the actual root of our centuries-old, all-American inability to get our shit together, no one can deny that the flinty survivors of Valley Forge embodied another national trait that every man, woman, and child in this republic is supposed to have: backbone, self-reliance, grit. An attribute that comes in handy in this less-than-public-spirited republic the Continentals were fighting to bring about.

As Theodore Roosevelt recalled of his asthmatic childhood, "I was nervous and timid. Yet reading of the people I admired," including, he says, "the soldiers of Valley Forge . . . I felt a great admiration for men who were fearless and who could hold their own in the world, and I had a great desire to be like them." Roosevelt grew up to be a more nuanced, competent president than that quotation implies. For all his rough-riding talk about the strenuous life, as a chief executive he operated under the assumption that perhaps the Federal Meat Inspection Act of 1906 might help a man hold his own in the world by making sure that even the most macho carnivore's bloody lunch comes out of a more hygienic slaughterhouse. Roosevelt somehow figured out how a manly American can try to live up to the Continentals' fortitude while at the same time becoming an elected official who tried to nurture a less fatal, more humane bureaucracy than the one responsible for the death toll at Valley Forge.

When Eisenhower gave his pep talk to the outdoorsy children camped at Valley Forge in 1950, he told them that in understanding the horrors of what went on there, "We turn to our own problems of today with increased confidence." Which is a stately way of saying that the only way to handle modern life's little setbacks in light of two thousand people being killed off in the winter of 1777 by starvation, disease, and administrative incompetence is to *suck it up, men*. (A mind-set consistently lampooned in the post-Vietnam era: "Sergeant, I think it's a bad idea to march today," said the army private played by Bill Murray in the 1981 film *Stripes*. "This *is* the cold and flu season.")

"Here at Valley Forge," Eisenhower said, "every relic, every monument assures us that even hunger, pain, nakedness and indescribable hardship cannot wholly dishearten those whose spirit is steeped in faith and in loyalty to a lofty purpose." A lesson, no doubt, some of the younger scouts would learn the hard way later on when squaring off against the stubborn idealists in the Vietcong.

Lafayette, astonished by the fortitude he witnessed at Valley Forge, reported that "the sacred fire of liberty burned on." Not that he could explain it. "The strength of that army," he wrote, "never ceased being a mystery."

"Military camp? More like a refugee camp," whispered my friend Wesley, the aforementioned musician and novelist husband of Abbey the sort-of-Quaker, as we watched a grim film of shivering, bedraggled Continental soldiers chopping down trees in a windy, frozen landscape. Shown in the visitor center at Valley Forge National Historic Park, the movie features the melody of a forlorn flute warbling under a narrator's bleak descriptions: *The routine of winter grew tiresome for the cold, hungry troops . . . Sickness reached epidemic proportions, fueled by poor sanitation and damp, overcrowded quarters.*

A few weeks after we went to Valley Forge, Wes mentioned, "That movie, with its endless shots of someone preparing a saucepan of gruel, has somewhat haunted me. If I want to try and make myself laugh, I imagine my life being directed by that terrible director of that terrible movie." I think the director's name was the Second Continental Congress?

The place itself, all green pastures, wide vistas, and blue sky, made less of an impression on Wes. Partly because ours was a cheerful outing on a nice spring day, but mostly because now Valley Forge is a national park, not a hellhole. In fact, according to the National Park Service, it "contains the largest area of meadows in southeastern Pennsylvania," making the park's five square miles "a refuge for grassland-dependent animals across the entire region."

Wes, an Englishman, finds the pleasant, pastoral terrain familiar, even homey.

"I'm from Hastings," he says. "The nearest train station to where I lived is called 'Battle.'" As in the Battle of Hastings of October 14, 1066, when forces commanded by the Norman duke soon to be nicknamed William the Conqueror defeated the army of King Harold II of England, who was killed that day, supposedly by being shot through the eye with an arrow or by being dismembered, or both.

Wes describes his boyhood landscape, like Valley Forge, as "a lot of empty land requiring a lot of imagining" in order to picture the place as it must have looked on that violent day almost a thousand years ago.

This all reminds me of how flummoxed I was when I read that Eisenhower retired in a house adjacent to the battlefield at Gettysburg. Wouldn't a general who had orchestrated so much carnage, I wondered, want to get as far away from bloodstained ground as he could? Then I went to Gettysburg. Most of it looks like a soccer field. I'm not using my imagination. I actually witnessed children playing soccer there. To find out about the fifty thousand men whose lives were lost or ruined in 1863 on what are now wide, welcoming expanses of grassland, the tourist (or the goalie) needs to read the National Park Service's signs.

Wes lives in nearby Mt. Airy, a stone's throw from Germantown. He has been to Cliveden, the impenetrable house where the Brits shot down so many rebels in the battle there in 1777. But he does seem more impressed that Germantown was the home of free jazz keyboard player and bandleader Sun Ra.

Because Wes lived in Brooklyn for many years, to him "Lafayette" was just the name of the subway stop at Lafayette Avenue. At his request, I rattled off the highlights of Lafayette's bio. He responded, "So you're writing about a Frenchman who got muddled up in a war on a continent far away from where he was from against a country very close to where he was from? It's like somebody from Ukraine battling Russia in Brazil."

I thought it would be fun to visit a Revolutionary War hotspot with a Brit, just to rub it in that we won, but Wes seemed too hazy on the subject to taunt. Afterward, we were talking about the park's grand triumphal arch, erected in 1917, which is inscribed with the names of Generals Lafayette, Greene, and De Kalb. He referred to it as "that big monument thing with all the Brooklyn streets."

I asked him if, when he was a boy in England, he had heard of Valley Forge. He said he had, but not at school. "There was a show on TV about Bob Hope entertaining the troops," he recalled. "Bob Hope said something like, 'Despite what you've been told, I did not entertain the troops at Valley Forge.'"

"Do not underestimate my ignorance about a war we were not really taught in England," he continued. "We concentrated on the wars we won—the First World War, the Second, the Tudors. Nobody taught me American history. Well, maybe a bit when we studied the Georges—there was always trouble off-stage in America. To us it was just the loss of a colony."

I guess the moral of that story is that no matter how many fireworks we set off to celebrate our forefathers throwing off the yoke of their colonial overlords, the overlords' descendants can't be bothered to remember, much less care, because they're still dining out on thwarting the Spanish Armada.

"It is a camp, in the centre of woods, fifteen hundred leagues from you," Lafayette wrote to his wife, Adrienne, from Valley Forge. He mentioned that the Frenchman he had asked to bring her the letter would describe the rustic circumstances her hus-

band had chosen to endure, instead of returning home to the comforts and pleasures of Paris, and how "honour alone told [him] to remain": "My presence is more necessary at this moment to the American cause, than you can possibly conceive," he wrote, given "some powerful cabals" plotting against Washington, who "would feel very unhappy if I were to speak of quitting him."

Despite all the challenges Washington had to deal with in designing and overseeing the construction of Valley Forge as Christmas came and went, his critics in the army and the Congress had not quieted down.

Inspector General Conway showed up at the camp, raring to inspect. Washington quickly sent him packing, explaining to Congress that he gave Conway the cold shoulder for the simple reason that "my feelings will not permit me to make professions of friendship to a man I deem my enemy."

Adding to Washington's torments, the Congress also rejiggered what had previously been a congressional committee, the Board of War. They appointed to it Washington's antagonists, Generals Horatio Gates and Thomas Mifflin, the officer gunning for Washington's job and the former quartermaster general enraged that Washington lost Philadelphia, respectively.

When not motivating his soldiers to slap up the log cabins they would spend the winter in and to dig their latrines, Washington made time to undermine the backstabbers, bringing to light Gates's and Conway's gossipy "weak general" letter shenanigans, which Congress officially frowned upon, even though a few of the delegates had said way worse.

In the end, it was Lafayette, not Washington, who bore the brunt of the cabal. Washington's rivals on the Board of War dispatched Lafayette to invade Canada—in winter, without providing the necessary personnel, supplies, or battle plan. "I go on very slowly," Lafayette wrote to Washington on his way north, "sometimes drenched by rain, sometimes covered by snow . . . if I am not starved I shall be as proud as if I had gained three battles." From Albany, he informed Washington that the undertaking was "madness," adding, "I have been deceived by the board of war."

The only upside to the pointless misadventure was a detour when Lafayette negotiated an alliance with the Oneida tribe in upstate New York, returning to Valley Forge with a cool new Indian name, Kayewla. Later that spring, a few dozen Oneida warriors even showed up at Valley Forge, ready to pitch in to help Kayewla and the patriot cause.

Lafayette frittered away his days in Albany writing letters to Washington about the absurdity of his no-go assignment: "I am afraid it will reflect on my reputation, and I shall be laughed at." In the meantime, a new arrival at Valley Forge was busy making the Continentals a less laughable fighting force.

Baron Friedrich Wilhelm von Steuben, a veteran of the Prussian army from the Seven Years' War, had served as a staff officer to the accomplished warrior King Frederick the Great. As Jay Luvaas writes of the monarch's hands-on approach to military leadership in *Frederick the Great on the Art of War*, "Often he could be seen on the drill ground, stop watch in hand, calculating the number of shots fired per minute." Luvaas adds, "Frederick once went so far as to claim that 'the speed with which the Prussian could reload trebled the firepower and made him the equal of three adversaries.'" Therefore, "by the variety and precision of its movements and the rapidity of its fire, the Prussian army soon came to enjoy a reputation comparable to that enjoyed by the Italians in music."

One of the countless European officers downsized after the Seven Years' War ended in 1763, Steuben then whiled away more than a decade as a court official in a minor principality in southwestern Germany. In the summer of 1777, his hopes of a new military commission in Baden were dashed when a rumor surfaced there that he had "taken familiarities with young boys."

With defense jobs on the Continent already scarce, the prospects for an aging veteran saddled with the unsubstantiated yet frowned upon accusation of being a homosexual were even gloomier. And so, like Lafayette, Steuben looked to the New World for employment. Yet unlike France's richest teenage orphan, the forty-six-year-old Steuben was broke.

Desperate, Steuben journeyed to Paris to meet with Benjamin Franklin and Silas Deane. By then the American commissioners were under strict orders from Congress not to sign up any more European recruits. But they could not ignore the fact that this one had served in what was arguably Europe's best-trained army.

Though they could not offer Steuben a commission, Franklin and Deane did provide him with a letter of introduction to Washington, dropping the name of French foreign minister

Vergennes as one of Steuben's admirers, plus enumerating (and exaggerating) his military accomplishments, instantly promoting him from Prussian army captain to lieutenant general.

Speaking of embellishment, the notion that Steuben also fudged his nobility by calling himself a baron has dogged his legacy for centuries. I tend to believe Steuben's adept biographer Paul Lockhart, who notes that Steuben, whose godfather was none other than the king of Prussia, was "nobly born." But more to the point, who cares? Though the story I'm telling necessitates typing reams of irritating words like "marquis," "duke," and, worst of all, "lord," at this point the only useful aristocratic title belongs to the Count on *Sesame Street*. Every time I come across a historian in a snit about Baron von Steuben not being a real baron, I am reminded of Theodore Roosevelt's exasperation at making small talk with all the royal muckety-mucks at the funeral of Edward VII: "I felt if I met another king I should bite him!"

Whether or not Steuben was a bona fide gentleman, he could not have gotten to America without assistance from a fake one. The playwright Beaumarchais—a watchmaker's son, né Caron, who had fabricated his fancy name and a phony coat of arms to go with it—came to Steuben's rescue. He lent Steuben money for travel expenses and offered him passage across the Atlantic on one of his Hortalez & Company ships.

Steuben sailed from France on September 26, 1777, without a guarantee that the flailing Continentals, recently walloped at Brandywine, would even take him. Night after night he must have stared out at the cold sea with a little hope and a lot of dread, contemplating the mystery fate awaiting him onshore. Which makes the bouncy scene depicting Chicago's annual Von Steuben Day parade in *Ferris Bueller's Day Off* all the merrier. Who could have predicted that more than two hundred years after this washed-up Teutonic mercenary bummed a ride across the Atlantic because he had nowhere else to go, the director of *Pretty in Pink* would hire the kid from *WarGames* to play a high school student who skips school and crashes a German-American celebration in Steuben's honor, commandeering a float of buxom Bavarians to lip-synch to Wayne Newton's "Danke Schoen."

After Steuben docked in New Hampshire in December, he stopped in Boston and then continued to York to hit up Congress for a job. En route, he forwarded Deane and Franklin's note to Washington and offered the commander his services as a volunteer, proclaiming, "The Object of my greatest Ambition is to render your Country all the Services in my Power, and to deserve the title of a Citizen of America by fighting for the Cause of your Liberty."

Which sounded a lot better than the truth: his pockets were empty and he was probably hoping to get hired before the Americans got wind of the gay thing. Though the *Advocate* magazine once referred to Steuben with a wink as "a lifelong bachelor," if he was in fact a homosexual, his life as a soldier would have ended if anyone found out. As Randy Shilts points out in *Conduct Unbecoming*, his book on gays and lesbians in the armed forces of the United States, the newly arrived Steuben may have witnessed a lieutenant court-martialed for sodomy get drummed out of Valley Forge. Literally: Washington ordered drummers and fifers to badger the man from the camp, making him "the first known soldier to be dismissed from the U.S. military for homosexuality."

Congress granted Steuben the temporary rank of captain. Aside from the letter from Franklin and Deane mentioning his military accomplishments and Vergennes's tacit support, it no doubt helped Steuben's cause that he looked the part. Before departing Paris, he had had an imposing Prussian-style officer's uniform made. A teenage private at Valley Forge later compared him to Mars, "the ancient fabled God of War." He noted, "The trappings of his horse, the enormous holsters of his pistols, his large size, and his strikingly martial aspect, all seemed to favor the idea."

The delegates also granted Steuben's request for commissions for some of his shipmates, as well as a pair of Frenchmen recruited by Beaumarchais whom Steuben had met in Boston, one of whom was the artist and engineer Pierre Charles L'Enfant. Thus in one slapdash human resources meeting, the congressmen not only hired the foreigner who would reshape the army, but as an afterthought also rubber-stamped the foreigner who would one day design the street plan of the future nation's capital, including the hilltop spot for a "Congress House" that became the Capitol building. Which sounds like a lucky turn of events until one remembers that to L'Enfant's new bunkmates at Valley Forge, snagging a potential city planner was not as fortunate as scoring a few bonus wagonloads of ham.

Upon arrival at Valley Forge in February of 1778, Steuben surmised, "No European army could have been kept together under such dreadful deprevation."

To remedy the supply problems, Washington had appointed Nathanael Greene as the new quartermaster general—much to Greene's dismay. "No body ever heard of a quarter Master in History," he complained, but he was good at it, and as winter turned to spring, his foraging parties had the campers who hadn't died or deserted better fed.

Washington invited Steuben to evaluate the state of the army, and Steuben made it clear there was room for improvement. To Washington's credit he welcomed the critique, putting Steuben in charge of retraining the troops.

According to Washington, "The Importance of establishing a Uniform System of useful Manoevres and regularity of discipline must be obvious, the Deficiency of our Army in these Respects must be equally so." Alas, he added, "the time we shall probably have to introduce the necessary Reformation is short."

Washington had also been ruminating on a deeper, less obvious stumbling block than the fact that summer—and summer battle season—was coming all too soon. Namely, that the rebels under his command were not fighting to become free; they were cornered into fighting because the government of Great Britain had failed to understand that they already were. As John Adams would recall in 1818, "But what do we mean by the American Revolution? Do we mean the American War?

The Revolution was effected before the War commenced. The Revolution was in the minds and hearts of the people." Yet the self-respect and self-possession that incited said people to revolt was hindering the revolution's goal, independence, because functional armies required hierarchy and self-denial, orders barked and orders followed.

Coming up with a catchy call to arms like "Give me liberty or give me death" requires different skills than actually bearing arms as a group does, especially in the technical context of eighteenth-century warfare. Who knows how many New World nonconformists actually did get death on the battlefield for the simple boring reason that their more conformist Old World enemies had been drilled ad nauseam on how to reload their muskets faster or how to wield their bayonets when there wasn't time to reload.

"Men accustomed to unbounded freedom, and no control," Washington wrote, "cannot brook the Restraint which is indispensably necessary to the good order and Government of an Army; without which, licentiousness, and every kind of disorder triumphant reign."

Steuben's new friend and Washington's aide de camp John Laurens wrote to his congressman father, "We want some kind of general Tutoring . . . so much."

Steuben caught on quick that he was dealing with an entirely new kind of man. As he would later describe these inherently insubordinate individuals to an officer crony back home in Prussia, "The genius of this nation is not to be compared . . .

with that of the Prussians, Austrians, or the French." (The genius for following orders, he meant.) Steuben explained to his friend, "You say to your soldier, 'Do this,' and he does it; but I am obliged to say, 'This is the reason why you ought to do that,' and *then* he does it."

At first, 120 soldiers were chosen to train under Steuben directly. "I made this guard my military school," he wrote. "I drilled them myself twice a day, and to remove that English prejudice which some officers entertained, namely, that to drill a recruit was a sergeant's duty and beneath the station of an officer, I often took the musket myself to show the men that manual exercise which I wished to introduce." Nearly three years after the war began, someone had finally gotten around to teaching the Continentals "to carry arms, stand at ease, present arms, to load, take aim, fire by platoons, and to charge bayonets." Steuben later recalled that before his bayonet lessons, "the American soldier, never having used this arm, had no faith in it, and never used it but to roast his beefsteak."

Steuben's show-and-tell method worked. "I had my company of guards exactly as I wished them to be," he gushed. "They were well dressed, their arms cleaned and in good order, and their general appearance quite respectable." He then "dispersed by apostles," sending the new, improved soldiers from his model company to fan out throughout the camp and preach the good news to their fellows.

Camp life, wrote Private Joseph Martin, became "a continual drill."

Impressed, Washington, in probably his most blatant defiance of the Continental Congress, promoted Steuben to be the Continental Army's inspector general. This did not sit well with the army's actual inspector general, the one the Congress had appointed a few weeks earlier.

"I am told that Baron Steuben is now in possession of the same place to which I was appointed," Inspector General Conway griped to General Gates. "I can venture to say that I would have effected in one Month or six Weeks, what he will not be able to accomplish in six Months."

Crowed Steuben, "I applied my system to battalions, afterwards to brigades and in less than three weeks, I executed maneuvers with an entire division in [the] presence of the commander in chief."

Who can blame Thomas Conway for thinking he could have been a better inspector general than Steuben? Or Horatio Gates for believing he could have out-generaled Washington? Conway and Gates were the surer bets—on paper.

Steuben went on to write a training manual the army kept in print through the War of 1812. In a passage about a commanding officer's duty regarding "the instruction of his recruits," he wrote, "that is a service that requires not only experience, but a patience and temper not met with in every officer." In other words, a commanding officer is a *person*. That Steuben, who needed a translator, what with his English vocabulary consisting almost entirely of swear words, ended up being the perfect hire to upgrade the Continental Army should rattle every search committee, small-business owner, casting director, college admissions officer, headhunter, and voter.

John Laurens admired Steuben because he "seems to understand what our Soldiers are capable of . . . He will not give us the perfect instructions absolutely speaking, but the best which we are in condition to receive."

Washington wrote to the Congress, "I should do injustice, if I were to be longer silent with regard to the merits of Baron Steuben." Convinced, Congress made Steuben's appointment as inspector general official, as well as promoting him to the rank of major general.

After Beaumarchais learned of Steuben's promotion, he wrote in a letter, "I congratulate myself on having given so great an officer to my friends, the free men . . . I am not by any means uneasy about the money I lent him for his voyage. Never did I make an investment that gave me so much pleasure, for I put a man of honor in the right place." (Good thing, too. Steuben never did pay back the playwright.)

The so-called Conway cabal was kaput. Ultimately, Conway quit and returned to France. General Gates resigned from the Board of War, eventually resuming a field command, overseeing one of the Continental Army's worst flops at Camden, South Carolina, in 1780. If there is anything to be learned from the conspiracy—other than when in doubt, bet on George Washington—it is to beware the pitfalls of certainty. Men like Benjamin Rush who were so sure in 1777 that Gates should replace Washington were sighing with relief three years later that they had not gotten their way. By 1780, Gates's reputation was in tatters, whereas Washington was clearly going places—the kind of places that would one day find Rush himself begging Washington's biographers to edit out his acerbic post-Brandy-wine complaints.

Lafayette was recalled to Valley Forge. "My only desire is to join you," he purred in a letter to Washington.

So he was back at the Pennsylvania camp with his division of Virginians that May when Simeon Deane, brother of Silas, galloped into Valley Forge with news: the French government had officially recognized the independence of the United States. Washington read aloud a letter Franklin and Deane sent from Paris: "We have now the great satisfaction of acquainting you and the Congress that the Treaties with France are at length completed and signed. The first is a treaty of amity and commerce . . . the other is a treaty of alliance."

Lafayette wept. Then he hugged Washington. Washington, I'm guessing, blushed.

Simeon Deane brought another letter for Lafayette from his wife. As laughter and huzzahs swirled around him, he read the news from Adrienne that their daughter Henriette had died.

"The loss of our poor child is almost constantly in my thoughts," he wrote to Adrienne. "This sad news followed immediately that of the treaty; and while my heart was torn by grief, I was obliged to receive and take part in expressions of public joy."

Steuben's French shipmate Pierre-Étienne Du Ponceau reported, "I thought I should be devoured by the caresses which the American officers lavished upon me as one of their new allies."

Writing to his congressman father about the ceremonial rifle salute performed by the troops at Valley Forge to celebrate the French alliance, John Laurens gushed about "the beautiful effect of the running fire which was executed to perfection." Columns of men led by Generals Lafayette and Stirling formed crisp lines, shooting their muskets in a rapid sequence called a *feu de joie*, a fire of joy, a feat of discipline and coordination unthinkable before Steuben's tutorials. "Long live the King of France!" they yelled.

Negotiating in Paris in the wake of French excitement about the victory at Saratoga (as well as their admiration for Washington's gutsy mishap at Germantown), Benjamin Franklin, Silas Deane, and Arthur Lee, representing "the Thirteen United States of America," had signed the Treaty of Alliance with "His Most Christian Majesty King Louis the Sixteenth" on February 6.

Both nations pledged "not to lay down their arms, until the independence of the United States shall have been formally or tacitly assured by the treaty or treaties that shall terminate the war." The starched language of diplomacy sounds so frumpy and therefore traditional that the reader almost forgets that this deeply weird partnership was history's first military pact between an absolute monarch and anti-monarchist republicans.

On March 20, the American envoys were summoned to the Château de Versailles. Though Benjamin Franklin left his famous fur cap at home and wore a nice enough brown velvet suit, an eyewitness at the palace divulged, "I should have taken him for a big farmer, so great was his contrast with the other diplomats, who were all powdered in full dress, and splashed all over with gold and ribbons."

Once the septuagenarian Franklin was ushered into the twenty-three-year-old king's chamber, Louis asked him, "Please assure Congress of my friendship."

Franklin promised the king that he could "count on the gratitude of Congress."

Louis remarked, "I hope this will be for the good of the two countries."

He hoped. It's not as though either man could make an educated guess about how this sort of coalition usually works out. They couldn't exactly look up what happened the last time the son of a Boston soap maker was in cahoots with the crowned head of the House of Bourbon. Sometimes there is something new under the sun, or, in this case, under the woefully bedazzled ceilings of a grotesque hunting lodge gone wrong.

Franklin, knowing how much courtesy mattered at court, flattered the king, "If all monarchies were governed by the principles which are in your heart, Sire, republics would never be formed."

I reread the previous tricky sentence at least thirty-eight times, and I still can't decide if Franklin actually meant it, considering the principles in Louis XVI's heart had more to do with sticking it to the British for snatching Quebec from his grandfather. What is obvious is that the patriots lucked out having a cagey old pro like Franklin doing their bidding chez Louis. What a relief that our first official diplomat knew a

VON STEUBEN

thing or two about being diplomatic, considering that back home Steuben was lecturing the inexperienced recruits at Valley Forge about how that pointy knife thing attached to their musket barrels was more than just a skewer to barbecue kebabs.

Over a decade after the Treaty of Alliance was signed, in the early days of the French Revolution, a forlorn Louis XVI would answer a letter from his Indian ally Tipu Sultan of Mysore, who was seeking French help in his war with the forces of Britain's East India Company under the command of our old pal Cornwallis. (This conflict on the subcontinent, by the way, became a footnote in U.S. history when the Mysoreans' missiles intrigued a British Army engineer, who went on to design his own versions for the redcoats, including those fired by the British fleet at Fort McHenry in 1814 and witnessed by Francis Scott Key, who immortalized "the rockets' red glare" in our national anthem, thus proving that the hippie saps are right and we really are all connected—by weaponry.) Anyway, Louis replied to the sultan, "This occasion"—being hit up for money, men, and arms to combat his old nemeses the British—"greatly resembles the American affair of which I never think without regret. On that occasion, they took advantage of my youth, and today we are paying the price for it."

The most influential member of this "they" who talked Louis into the alliance with the Americans was undoubtedly his foreign minister Vergennes. After Franklin's audience with the king, the treaty celebrations at Versailles culminated in a dinner hosted by Vergennes with Franklin seated next to him in the chair that traditionally had been reserved for the British ambassador. Nearly three years after Vergennes's spy in Philadelphia gave Franklin vague assurances that France wished the rebels well, Franklin and Vergennes could finally rejoice in person, and more important, in public.

In the months between the signing of the Franco-American Treaty of Alliance on February 6, 1778, and its ratification by the Continental Congress on May 4, Britain declared war on France. At the same time, British prime minister Lord North also spearheaded a last-ditch effort at reconciliation with the colonies. North dispatched a doomed "peace commission" to meet with Congress and delivered an address to the House of Commons on February 17 suggesting that the British government should capitulate on all the Americans' prewar sticking points, except for recognizing independence. His hope, however faint, was that the colonists would go back to being subjects of the crown if the Coercive Acts were repealed, Parliament gave up the right to tax the colonies, the Continental Congress was recognized as "a legal body," and Americans were allowed to elect members of the House of Commons. According to a contemporary periodical's coverage of this speech, the MPs' reaction to these suggestions was "a dull melancholy silence," then "astonishment, dejection and fear."

What a waste. The previous twelve years of bad blood and corpses could have been avoided if these same astonished and dejected men had paid attention to Ben Franklin's testimony about the Stamp Act before the House of Commons back in 1766. He acknowledged that while at that moment Britain "will not find a rebellion" in her colonies, he warned the members of Parliament that if their unjust laws were enforced at gunpoint, "they may, indeed, make one."

There was no going back. "Nothing short of Independence," Washington wrote to Henry Laurens, "can possibly do." Of course the Continental Congress of the United States ratified the Treaty of Alliance with the nation that recognized the United States. "What they call in France, my new country," cheered Lafayette.

But before we cue the brass section to blare "The Stars and Stripes Forever," it might be worth taking another moment of melancholy silence to mourn the thwarted reconciliation with the mother country and what might have been. Anyone who accepts the patriots' premise that all men are created equal must come to terms with the fact that the most obvious threat to equality in eighteenth-century North America was not taxation without representation but slavery. Parliament would abolish slavery in the British Empire in 1833, thirty years before President Lincoln's Emancipation Proclamation. A return to the British fold in 1778 might have freed American slaves three decades sooner, which is what, an entire generation and a half? Was independence for some of us more valuable than freedom for all of us? As the former slave Frederick Douglass put it in an Independence Day speech in 1852, "This is your Fourth of July, not mine."

You know your country has a checkered past when you find yourself sitting around pondering the humanitarian upside of sticking with the British Empire.

. . .

Ah, spring. May 1778, specifically. Coming up on cannon weather. But then who needs to pay for gunpowder when heatstroke kills for free?

William Howe would soon sail home, leaving his number two, Henry Clinton, as the new commander in chief. Ordered by Germain to evacuate Philadelphia and return to the British stronghold of New York City, Clinton skipped town the morning of May 18, leading an exodus across the Delaware River of more than fifteen thousand British and Hessian troops, three thousand Loyalist Philadelphians, and fifteen hundred wagons of supplies and sundries. With an unwieldy, twelve-mile-long caravan of sweaty slowpokes inching across New Jersey for weeks on end, Clinton was pretty much asking to be attacked.

In June Washington convened a couple of war councils to seek his generals' advice on whether or not to hit Clinton from behind. Greene and Steuben were in favor. Ditto Anthony Wayne, who hoped to repeat the Saratoga surrender of Johnny Burgoyne by "Burgoyning Clinton." In his memoirs Lafayette claimed that he "asserted that it would be disgraceful for the chiefs, and humiliating for the troops, to allow the enemy to traverse the Jerseys tranquilly; that, without running any improper risk, the rear guard might be attacked."

In the bronze bas-relief sculpture depicting one of these meetings that's on the nineteenth-century monument in front of the Monmouth County courthouse in Freehold, New Jersey, Lafayette leans over a table with a map on it, goading Washing-

CLINTON

ton on. The other generals appear convinced, except for an ever-so-skeptical Henry Knox, who grips a sword as if he's fantasizing about stabbing Lafayette with it, and General Charles Lee, who scowls with his arms crossed with an invisible but implied thought bubble above his head saying, *Harrumph.*

Lee had recently been returned to the Continentals at Valley Forge through a prisoner exchange. He was, technically, Washington's second in command. The two had served together in the French and Indian War. An Englishman hailing from Cheshire, Lee spent nearly twenty years as an officer in His Majesty's army before retiring and settling in Virginia in 1773. The more experienced Lee had expected the Continental Congress to appoint him commander in chief of the Continental Army back in '75. He never really got over Washington getting the job instead. In 1776 Washington had one of the Continentals' Hudson River forts renamed after him, which is how the city of Fort Lee, New Jersey, got its name.

Soon thereafter Lee was captured when the British tracked him to his lodgings in a country tavern, yanking him out in his bathrobe and slippers. He spent over a year as Manhattan's most pampered POW, being wined and dined nightly in comfortable, officer-worthy digs while his patriot comrades jailed on the prison ships in the East River were getting their dietary protein by licking the lice off their hands.

Washington had his suspicions that Lee might have gotten treasonously cozy with his old redcoat coworkers. Eight decades would pass before someone nosing through the papers of William Howe's secretary in 1857 found a document proving Lee's collaboration with the British. A page with Lee's advice to Howe on how to take and hold Philadelphia was labeled "Mr. Lee's plan, March 29, 1777."

In June of '78, once Washington made the decision to attack Clinton at Monmouth, he offered Lee the command of the advance guard's five thousand troops. Qualms or not, Lee had seniority. Lee declined, deeming it beneath him, more the purview of a "young, volunteering general." Having a particularly puppyish one of those on hand, Washington offered the command to Lafayette. According to the diary of one of his aides, Lafayette was "in raptures with his command and burning to distinguish himself." Then Lee wanted it back. Then Washington reminded Lee his heart wasn't in it. Then Lee agreed and backed off. Then he changed his mind yet again. Washington threw up his hands and told Lafayette to proceed. Lee wrote to Washington to complain that if he were usurped by a junior officer, he would be "disgraced." Lafayette was a good sport and wrote to Washington, "If it is believed necessary or useful to the good of the service and the honour of General Lee . . . I will cheerfully obey and serve him." Alexander Hamilton wrote, "General Lee's conduct with respect to the command of this corps was truly childish." In the end, Washington followed protocol, deciding to let Lee lead the first wave of Continentals. Washington ordered Lee to attack Clinton's rear guard.

The morning of June 28, Washington kept an ear out for the sound of Lee's artillery. Hearing neither cannon nor mortar, only the occasional forlorn musket pop, Washington rode toward Monmouth to find out what the holdup was. Quizzing the torrent of Continentals who started coming toward him, Washington determined that Lee had ordered a retreat before much of the corps had even begun to execute his instructions to advance.

Washington, fuming, spotted Lee. Uninterested in Lee's excuses for calling off the attack, Washington yelled, "Go to the rear, sir." As Lee rode off, Washington let rip a spew of profanity.

General Charles Scott of Virginia, who had served with both Washington and Lee in the French and Indian War, claimed to hear the whole thing, getting a kick out of His Excellency's meltdown: "Yes, sir, he swore on that day till the leaves shook on the trees. Charming! Delightful! Never have I enjoyed such swearing, before or since. Sir, on that memorable day, he swore like an angel from Heaven."

Afterward, Lee was court-martialed and found guilty of disobeying orders, disrespecting the commander in chief, and "misbehavior before the enemy . . . by making an unnecessary, disorderly, and shameful retreat." Lee was suspended from duty for a year, but his response to that was to send the Congress an offensive letter that insulted the delegates into booting him out for good.

In 2014, a scandal nicknamed "Bridgegate" outraged the tri-state area when news broke that the New Jersey governor's deputy chief of staff allegedly ordered politically motivated, arbitrary lane closures on the George Washington Bridge at rush hour. The deputy e-mailed a colleague, "Time for some traffic problems in Fort Lee." The resulting traffic jams, meant to inconvenience commuters crossing the Hudson River, were reportedly acts of retribution against the mayor of Fort Lee for declining to endorse the governor in the gubernatorial election. There is an ongoing investigation as I write this. But no matter the outcome, the most important question this purported abuse of power brought to light is obvious: Why is Fort Lee still named Fort Lee?

Even setting aside the probability of Lee's treason that was uncovered in 1857, surely getting kicked out of a struggling army that could not afford to be terribly picky about who was in it was grounds for renaming Fort Lee back in the day. Changing Hudson River fort names after personnel shake-ups was not unprecedented at the time. For instance, the patriots were quick to rechristen the New York citadel they had named after General Benedict Arnold once his treason was exposed, which is how Fort Arnold became Fort Clinton and then West Point.

The scene of Washington cussing out Charles Lee was for some reason not included in the series of bronze illustrations of the Battle of Monmouth on the monument at the county courthouse. Even though it was the most New Jersey–like behavior in the battle, if not the entire war.

What happened next is most definitely carved in bronze on the Monmouth monument and worth a look-see for passersby on their way to drug court. A dynamic account titled "Washington Rallying the Troops" pictures the commander on horseback, in flight. Washington shouts orders midair at some musket-wielding infantrymen. Unlike the horse, the grunt in the foreground is not wearing shoes. He's not wearing a hat either, but only because he has taken it off to cheer his commander in chief. Washington's coat and the horse's tail bounce behind him as he points his sword to the future.

Sir Henry Clinton spared Washington the chore of chasing him. When Lee approached Clinton's rear guard earlier that morning, the redcoats were waiting for him. When Lee fled, Clinton and Cornwallis pursued. So Washington was not rallying his retreating troops to turn around and go back to the front. He was convincing them to stand and fight because the front had followed them.

"His presence stopped the retreat," recounted Lafayette. "His graceful bearing on horseback, his calm and deportment which still retained a trace of displeasure . . . were all calculated to inspire the highest degree of enthusiasm." He added, "I thought then as now that I had never beheld so superb a man."

Hamilton remarked, "I never saw the general to so much advantage. His coolness and firmness was admirable."

The real story of Monmouth was the troops' newfound cool, the payoff of Steuben's drills at Valley Forge. "After they recovered from the first surprise occasioned by the retreat of the advanced corps," Washington later wrote to the Congress, the army's performance the rest of the day "could not be surpassed."

General Wayne took charge of Lee's retreating regiments, holding off the advancing Brits as Washington regrouped the main army behind him.

Greene would have the kind of gratifying day that only comes with comeuppance. Nine months earlier he was called on to cover his comrades' panicked flight after Cornwallis spooked them at Brandywine. At Monmouth, Greene, backed up by a line of artillery positioned on a hill above him, led the Continentals, who repeatedly rebuffed elite infantry directed by Cornwallis himself.

One of the panels on the monument depicts Molly Pitcher, who was either an actual woman named Mary Hays or a tall tale or the composite of a lot of actual women including one named Mary Hays (or not) at different battles. Which is to say that Molly Pitcher was a folk hero. The story goes that during the Battle of Fill in the Blank, "Molly Pitcher," an artillery-man's wife, was fetching buckets of water for her spouse's cannon crew to drink and to dampen the swabs they plunged into the barrel between firings to snuff out any burning embers before cramming in the next round of gunpowder. When her wounded husband fell down dead, she stepped in and took his place on the crew. One colorful version of the tale has an enemy cannonball ripping her dress as it flew between her knees, but she shrugged it off, pointing out that things could have gone worse.

Since she may or may not have existed, there is more than one probably phony "Molly Pitcher's spring," the well where she allegedly drew her water. Before swinging by the monument at the county courthouse, my friend Jonathan Sherman and I spot a couple of Molly Pitcher's spring contenders, one in Monmouth Battlefield State Park and another next to some railroad tracks nearby.

On the courthouse monument, Molly is front and center, a determined dame in a swirling frock shoving a rammer down the barrel of a cannon. A dead man, presumably Mr. Molly, lies on the ground near her feet. Henry Knox lurks off to the side.

I mention to Sherm that there's a rumor the sculptor, James Edward Kelly, used a young Thomas Edison as a model for one of the artillerymen standing behind Molly. Sherm takes out his phone and retrieves a photo of Thomas Edison to see if any of the men in Molly's vicinity resemble the inventor. By that, I do not mean that he calls up Edison's picture from the Internet. He has an Edison portrait on his phone already, in between snapshots of his kids.

When I ask him why he has a photo of Edison handy, he replies, "I have lots of pictures of Edison on my phone. I find him inspiring." He reminds me not to underestimate how much people from New Jersey love talking about famous people from New Jersey. Sherm was born in Morristown and grew up in Livingston, though it would have been impolite to point out that Edison, the "Wizard of Menlo Park," was born in Ohio but grew up in Michigan.

Sherm holds up the Edison photo next to the monument, looking for a resemblance. He even compares the visage of the dead husband lying at Molly Pitcher's feet to another picture of an elderly Edison in the same pose, taking a nap outdoors as two buddies sit nearby reading the paper.

The main reason he keeps the Edison pictures handy, Sherm says, is for pep talks with his seven-year-old son, Sam. "I like bringing him up in an ongoing conversation with Sam about Edison's formula for genius of ninety-nine percent perspiration and one percent inspiration and why it shouldn't be flipped and turned into one percent perspiration as Sam would like it to be." This seems like a more constructive use of historical figures to chasten children than the shivering soldiers of Valley Forge shaming an asthmatic little Teddy Roosevelt into weight lifting.

There was literal and figural perspiration aplenty at the Battle of Monmouth. The temperature was upwards of one hundred degrees. "The mouth of a heated oven seemed to me to be but a trifle hotter than this ploughed field," recalled Joseph Plumb Martin. Around a third of the day's casualties would die of plain old heatstroke, including George Washington's horse.

The Continentals fought until dusk, pushing back each enemy advance until Clinton bailed, conducting his men back toward the village of Monmouth Courthouse and out of range of Knox's artillery.

"We forced the Enemy from the Field," Washington wrote to Henry Laurens, "and encamped on the Ground." Intending to resume the battle at first light, the living slept there among the dead. Washington spread his cloak under an apple tree, stretching out next to Lafayette. Like boys at a sleepover, they gossiped about Charles Lee until drifting off.

Come morning, Washington discovered that Clinton had set decoy campfires to trick him into believing they would resume the engagement at sunup. But Clinton had stolen away in the dark, marching his army to Sandy Hook. Royal Navy transport boats were waiting there to ferry them to Manhattan and safety.

Before Sherm and I drive back to New York, we stop at one more historic site in Freehold, the former home of some twentieth-century relatives of one Private John Springsteen, who volunteered with the Monmouth County militia in 1775. This is the modest clapboard duplex at 39½ Institute Street where Bruce Springsteen was living on September 9, 1956, the night he watched Elvis Presley's first appearance on *The Ed Sullivan Show.*

After the broadcast, the six-year-old Springsteen talked his mother into renting him a guitar, "inspired," he later recalled, "by the passion in Elvis' pants." (The pants always get a lot of play, and for good reason, but when I went back to the clips of "Hound Dog" and "Ready Teddy," I was just as mesmerized by the carnal hilarity of Presley's facial expressions—the finest eyebrow work since Groucho Marx.)

In a speech Springsteen delivered in Texas in 2012, he boiled down what he had learned that night from Elvis: "You did not have to be constrained by your upbringing, by the way you looked, or by the social context that oppressed you. You could call upon your own powers of imagination, and you could create a transformative self."

Later, I e-mail Sherm to thank him for indulging me in that last stop. I was under the impression that he preferred our time at the museum in Monmouth Battlefield State Park, with me talking at him about the significance of Friedrich von Steuben's army training manual on display there.

"Not only was stopping at one of Springsteen's childhood homes appropriate," Sherm replies, "it was an important part of the day for me as a Jersey boy, since it served as a great reminder that not all important fights take place on battlefields. Some take place in tiny houses, or half-houses, whether with family members or within oneself, and involve changing your course, convincing your mother to rent you a guitar (or my father to buy me a typewriter), and getting the hell out of that house, that town, that state. It's a different kind of independence, personal instead of political, but one of the many things we won in that war fought over two centuries ago turned out to be the freedom of expression that let a dude from Jersey write a song like 'Thunder Road.'"

The morning after the Battle of Monmouth, Washington's orders had gushed, "The Commander in Chief congratulates the army on the victory obtained over the arms of his Britannic Majesty yesterday and thanks most sincerely the gallant officers and men who distinguished themselves upon the occasion."

To Washington it was a victory. To nitpickers and spoilsports, it was more of a draw. The British did not so much retreat as achieve their objective of moving from Philadelphia to New York. Whether or not the Continentals won, they did not lose. If it was a draw, it was a respectable one. Steuben's training had made the army more professional, coordinated, and skilled. After the morning's Charles Lee hiccup, Washington, his officers, and the enlisted men worked in concert to right the ship. At last Washington could ask the question about whether these were the men with whom he must defend America and the answer might actually cheer him up.

In August, a few weeks after Monmouth, Washington was ensconced in new headquarters in White Plains, New York. He was there to keep a threatening eye on Clinton, who was holed up in Manhattan daydreaming about resigning from a post he would soon describe as "this mortifying command." The last time Washington had been in White Plains was during the "times that try men's souls" era of the New York campaign in '76.

"It is not a little pleasing, nor less wonderful to contemplate," Washington wrote to an old compatriot in the Virginia House of Burgesses, "that after two years maneuvering and undergoing the strangest vicissitudes that perhaps ever attended any one contest since the creation, both armies are brought back to the very point they set out from." Except the second time around, things were looking up. His nimbler, tougher Continentals had proven themselves to be worthier opponents, and the king of France had his back.

The rebels were so optimistic that France's entry into the war could only mean that the war was almost over, that when Steuben first heard the news of the French alliance back at Valley Forge, he sent Congressman Henry Laurens his congratulations, speculating, "I may not, perhaps, have an opportunity of drawing my sword in your cause."

Laurens's ominous reply: "There is blood, much blood in our prospect, and . . . there will be opportunity and incitement to unsheath your sword." Laurens, suspecting that Steuben was underestimating the tenacity of the pigheaded Anglo-Saxon islanders with whom they were at war, foretold, "Britain will not be humbled by a stroke of policy; she will be very angry, and if she is to fall, her fall will be glorious. We, who know her, ought to be prepared."

Laurens wrote those words on May 11, 1778. Which was three years and twenty-two days after the first shot at Lexington. And five years, three months, and twenty-two days until September 3, 1783, when Benjamin Franklin, John Adams, and John Jay would sign the treaty with Great Britain officially ending the war.

So in August of 1778, when George Washington was up in White Plains looking on the bright side, he had no clue that Monmouth would be the last battle he commanded in the north. In fact, the whole reason he was hunkered down in that particular Westchester County suburb—aside from just generally putting the screws on Henry Clinton—was to plan a grandiose campaign in which the French would help him take back New York. Never happened. Moreover, Washington would not personally command another battle for *three more years*.

The Revolutionary War's classic period ends at Monmouth. What a golden age of ideas and action that was! Remember when Jefferson got up out of his chair? And Henry Knox schlepped the cannons to Boston? And Paris fell for Franklin's fur hat and everything the hat implied? Remember that night under the apple tree at Monmouth, when Washington slept on the ground, with Lafayette curled up beside him? Remember when Elvis and his pants went on *Ed Sullivan*? Well, until the day an older, hungrier Washington puts on his black leather suit and gets the old band back together at Yorktown, we're going to have to fast-forward through a few years of "Do the Clam."

. . .

The physical manifestation of George Washington's frustration is my neighbor. I live in Manhattan near Union Square, where a statue of Washington on horseback gazes across Fourteenth Street a few yards away from a wistful likeness of Lafayette the boy sculpted by Frédéric-Auguste Bartholdi of Statue of Liberty fame. The Washington is not as sugary as the Lafayette, but when wasn't that true?

The big bronze commemorates Washington riding into New York City at war's end. November 25, 1783—the day the last of the redcoats finally abandoned New York for the first time since occupying it in 1776—was such a relief that New Yorkers celebrated Evacuation Day as a cherished November holiday for decades. That is, until Abraham Lincoln came along and ruined it. Him and his stupid Thanksgiving.

So Washington's equestrian likeness was meant to look triumphant, and it does. But then again, it's the picture of a dream denied. Washington never fantasized about trotting into town in an orderly fashion after diplomats hammered out a deal. He yearned to recapture the city in some flashy Franco-American amphibious show of strength, culminating in the transformation of Sir Henry Clinton's surname into a participle connoting humiliation like "getting Burgoyned."

The main reason the patriots had pushed for the French alliance was to get their hands on the French navy's enormous ships, vessels groaning under the weight of so much weaponry it was a wonder they stayed afloat. In July of 1778, a French fleet appeared off the Jersey shore, its four frigates and twelve ships of the line (including the ninety-gun flagship the *Languedoc*) commanded by Lafayette's cousin-in-law Admiral Charles Hector, Count d'Estaing.

Washington licked his lips anticipating a grandiose joint operation in New York that history would look back on as the day that Clinton got Clintoned. Until d'Estaing, estimating that a sandbar made the channel into New York Harbor too shallow for his largest deep-sea Death Stars to squeeze through, nixed that plan.

So Washington's dream was thwarted by math. At least that was d'Estaing's excuse. In his landmark study *The Influence of Sea Power on History*—the imperialism starter kit for Theodore Roosevelt's generation of warmongers—Alfred Thayer Mahan ruminates that d'Estaing "probably reasoned that France had nothing to gain by the fall of New York, which might have led to peace between America and England, and left the latter free to turn all her power against his own country. Less than that would have been enough to decide his wavering mind as to risking his fleet over the bar."

As much as any alleged geopolitical cunning, d'Estaing's "wavering mind" would be a deciding factor throughout this inaugural Franco-American campaign. That and the wind. A seasoned general (and therefore a confirmed landlubber), d'Estaing had been reappointed as an admiral by his chum the king. Which is why his sailors kept referring to him as "General" as a semi-snub. In fact, before putting the kibosh on a potentially conclusive attack on New York, d'Estaing had already goofed a potentially conclusive attack on Philadelphia, having put out from France with orders to blockade the Delaware Bay so as to trap the Howe brothers' army and navy near Philadelphia; but he dillydallied crossing the Atlantic and arrived after the enemy had evacuated the capital.

D'Estaing's timidity could be explained by simple lack of experience, especially when he was compared with Black Dick Howe, the human sea shanty he was up against. The older brother of the recently departed commander in chief General Sir William, Admiral Lord Richard Howe joined the Royal Navy at thirteen. Andrew O'Shaughnessy writes in *The Men Who Lost America*, "Howe pioneered the naval code of practice for amphibious warfare, in which the navy transported and gave logistical support to the army in beachhead landings." Theory and practice—Howe was the whole package. Despite the superior size and firepower of the French fleet, d'Estaing would have been insane not to dread him.

D'Estaing hailed from Lafayette's birthplace, Auvergne—a landlocked province that did not scream maritime potential. The presence of his fellow Auvergnat seemed to amplify Lafayette's homesickness, perhaps reminding him of Britain's role in his fatherless boyhood at Chavaniac. He egged on d'Estaing: "May you defeat them, sink them to the bottom, lay them as low as they have been insolent; may you begin the great work of their destruction by which we shall trample upon their nation; may you prove to them at their expense what a Frenchman, and a Frenchman from Auvergne, can do."

For months, Lafayette had been calling the United States

RICHARD HOWE

"my country," sending Adrienne talking points on what the "wife of an American officer" should say. The coming of d'Estaing's fleet Frenched him up considerably.

Washington, putting aside his New York revenge fantasy for the moment, convinced d'Estaing to sail north toward Narragansett Bay and occupied Rhode Island. The British had controlled Newport, on the southern coast of Aquidneck Island, since 1776. Half the city's residents had fled, abandoning hundreds of homes and businesses that the six thousand enemy troops, mostly Hessians, tore down to burn as firewood. Thankfully, Touro Synagogue, the country's oldest, still stands. To this day, it remains the grand symbol of Aquidneck Island's backstory as a refuge for Jews, Baptists, Quakers, and other outcasts from Puritan Massachusetts, like the Protestant heretic Anne Hutchinson.

After the war, in 1790, Newport's synagogue would go on to inspire one of Washington's finer moments as a president and person. Responding to a letter from Touro's Moses Seixas, who asked the new president if ratifying the Bill of Rights really was, to paraphrase, good for the Jews, Washington would send a letter addressed to the Hebrew Congregation at Newport. The First Amendment, he explained, exposed tolerance as a sham, because tolerance implies one superior group of people deigning to put up with their inferiors.

"It is now no more that toleration is spoken of as if it were the indulgence of one class of people that another enjoyed the exercise of their inherent natural rights," Washington wrote. "For, happily, the Government of the United States . . . gives to bigotry no sanction, to persecution no assistance."

Of course, before he could write that letter to Newport, Washington would have to pry the British out of Newport.

Washington sent Lafayette north with two thousand Continentals, who were to join up with the regional militiamen set to partner with d'Estaing. In his memoirs, Lafayette described their journey from White Plains to Providence "across a smiling country, covered with villages, in which the evident equality of the population distinctly proved the democracy of the government. From the apparent prosperity of each colony, it was easy to judge of the degree of freedom which its constitution might enjoy."

Nathanael Greene, who was to share command of the regulars with Lafayette, was the descendant of Quakers drawn to the misfit magnet that was colonial Rhode Island. He was in spasms of envy when the commander in chief assigned the more senior General John Sullivan of New Hampshire to lead the joint operation with the French in his home state. Greene congratulated Sullivan on being "the first General that has ever had an opportunity of cooperating with the French forces belonging to the United States." He added, "You are the most happy man in the World."

Sullivan's assignment required as much diplomacy as it did soldiering, which proved something of a challenge for a man Washington had recently reprimanded for his short fuse: "No other officer of rank in the whole army has so often conceived himself neglected, slighted, and ill-treated as you have done, and none, I am sure, has had less cause than yourself to entertain such ideas."

In fact, after Sullivan had chewed him out, Admiral D'Estaing noted in a report that Sullivan had been a lawyer before the war. D'Estaing speculated that he "must have been an uncomfortable man for his clients."

Convening in Rhode Island, Sullivan and d'Estaing quibbled from the get-go about which nation would have the honor of storming Newport first. They tabled this quandary when news of the Royal Navy's oncoming fleet made d'Estaing and his ships dash off to spar with Howe. Or that was the plan. They sailed straight into a storm instead. The tempest lasted three full days. Howe hustled back to New York. Winds bunted d'Estaing's ships so far from port that Sullivan brooded for over a week about his allies' fate. To Sullivan's relief, the Frenchmen finally returned. To Sullivan's dismay, this was more of a courtesy call. Having lost his flagship's masts and rudder, d'Estaing just swung by to alert Sullivan that he and his walloped flotilla would have to skip the Newport operation altogether and proceed forthwith to Boston for repairs.

To Sullivan, the only thing worse than attacking Newport with those godforsaken Frenchmen would be attacking Newport without them. Because the regional militias had heeded Sullivan's call for help, his forces had doubled to ten thousand troops, among them the starry Massachusetts militiamen and Sons of Liberty of yore John Hancock and Paul Revere. "It seems as if half of Boston was here," Revere wrote home. Because of d'Estaing—or as d'Estaing might see it, the weather—half of Boston was about to be trapped on an island less than three miles from six thousand enemies who might be reinforced at any moment by Admiral Howe or a whole other British fleet that had been spotted off Long Island.

Sullivan had Greene and Lafayette ferried to the *Languedoc* to try to convince d'Estaing to stay and fight.

"If we fail in our negotiation," Greene told Lafayette en route to d'Estaing's ship, "we shall at least get a good dinner." Washington should have chosen Greene, not Sullivan, to steer this mission. Besides his cool head and personal interest in helping his home state, Greene understood that whatever their shortcomings, the French could always be counted on to roast the hell out of a chicken.

Greene and Lafayette pleaded their case, but d'Estaing and his officers would not change their minds. They said their vessels were so damaged that a potential skirmish against one, much less two British squadrons would sink them for sure. However, d'Estaing invited Greene to stick around and make his case in writing.

"The expedition against Rhode Island was undertaken upon no other consideration than that of the French fleet and troops acting in concert with the American troops," stressed Greene. If the French were to forsake them, the mission would be in vain, causing "a great discontent and murmuring among the people." D'Estaing was unmoved.

Lafayette wrote to Washington that d'Estaing had received clear orders from Louis XVI "to go to Boston in case of an accident or a superior fleet." D'Estaing, he said, suffered "true affliction not being able to assist America."

The next day Sullivan convened a council of war. Greene

and Lafayette attended. Everyone but Lafayette helped craft a letter to d'Estaing threatening that France would be dishonored if the fleet deserted its ally "upon an Island the midst of an Expedition agreed to by the Count himself." Also, they warned, the fleet's withdrawal from Newport would injure the alliance between France and the United States. Greene signed the letter. The general of the Massachusetts militia also put his John Hancock on it. "I refused to sign," Lafayette declared.

In the meantime, d'Estaing had vanished. "The french," a colonel in the Second Rhode Island Regiment confided in his diary, "left us in a most Rascally manner."

Sullivan raged to Henry Laurens that d'Estaing's departure "has raised every voice against the French nation, revived all those ancient prejudices against the faith and sincerity of that people, and inclines them most heartily to curse the new alliance."

Lafayette took umbrage—just gobs and gobs of umbrage—at the patriots' vilification of his countrymen for leaving Newport. Here's hoping George Washington was in the mood for some long letters.

"It is not to the commander-in-chief, it is to my most dearest friend, General Washington, that I am speaking," Lafayette unburdened himself. "Frenchmen of the highest character have been exposed to the most disagreeable circumstances . . . I am more upon a warlike footing in the American lines than when I come near the British lines at Newport." So much for the "smiling country."

Lafayette's split loyalties tormented him. He confessed in a letter to Adrienne, "Half the Americans say that I am passionately fond of my country, and the other half say that since the arrival of the French ships, I have become mad . . . Betwixt ourselves, they are a little in the right; I never felt so strongly what may be called national pride."

Sullivan sent Lafayette to Boston to plead with d'Estaing to turn around and come back. D'Estaing was happy to see him, but the fleet stayed put.

Regardless of whether d'Estaing was justified in absconding to Boston, the fact remained that the whole point of targeting Newport in the first place was that the French fleet was supposed to make ganging up on the relatively modest British garrison there a snap. Which was how Sullivan had successfully recruited five thousand regional militiamen—overwhelming force, guaranteed win, no fuss. Without backup from the French fleet, a foregone conclusion had turned into possible suicide. Most of them took off for home, including Hancock and Revere.

Greene wrote to Washington that their troop levels were down to a "vexatious and truly mortifying" four thousand to five thousand men, a dangerous tally in light of the six thousand redcoats and Hessians a stone's throw away, not to mention the ever-present threat of the Royal Navy lending a hand.

On August 29, British and Hessian forces did harass the American withdrawal from the island. But considering the mercifully low death toll of thirty patriots—the potential for slaughter was in the hundreds—the engagement led by Sullivan and Greene on Aquidneck is mainly remembered for the solid performance of the First Rhode Island Regiment, a segregated Continental unit of freed slaves.

Lafayette missed out on the action in Rhode Island because he was still in Boston buttering up d'Estaing. So Congress presented him with a counterintuitive commendation apologizing for keeping him *out* of harm's way. They sure had his number. The resolution recognized "the sacrifice he made of his personal feelings, when, for the interest of the United States, he repaired to Boston, at the moment when the opportunity of acquiring glory of the field of battle would present itself."

In his patient, paternal reply to Lafayette's agitated letters, Washington explained, "I feel for you and for our good and great allies the French . . . and, lastly, I feel for my country." Reasonable people, he said, appreciated d'Estaing and his fleet's effort. Washington then unearthed the upside to the patriots' harsh appraisal of their allies: "In a free and republican government, you cannot restrain the voice of the multitude; every man will speak as he thinks, or, more properly, without thinking, and consequently will judge at effects without attending to the causes." Washington was reminding Lafayette that even though the establishment of a free and republican government comes with half-baked tomfoolery and half-cocked bile, every now and then someone who has something to say gets to say it.

In the end, the British held on to Newport, which Mahan credits to Admiral Howe's "energy and confidence in himself as a seaman." Mahan points out that if not for Howe, who had the guts to go after d'Estaing's bigger, better fleet, thereby drawing the French out to sea and into the storm that smacked them into submission, "the gale would not have saved the British force at Newport."

Howe's moves were more significant than the preservation of a specific British outpost. In fact, the British would willingly evacuate Newport the following year to consolidate their troops to conquer Charleston. Howe's nerve and poise had set in motion a rift between the Americans and the French that put the Franco-American alliance in danger. An alliance that was awkward from the start, not just because it was a partnership between republicans and monarchists but because of, as Sullivan put it, the Americans' "ancient prejudices" against the French. Prejudices that stretched back to the Norman conquest of England in 1066 and that were reawakened by the recent French and Indian War.

In *Common Sense*, which Washington ordered read aloud to Continental troops in Boston after it was published in January of 1776, Thomas Paine took aim at William the Conqueror in his enumeration of arguments against "the evil of monarchy . . . and that of hereditary seccession." Regarding the claim of divine right by the royal heirs of the Norman invader, Paine carped, "A French bastard landing with an armed banditti, and establishing himself king of England against the consent of the natives, is in plain terms a very paltry rascally original. It certainly hath no divinity in it."

What if Howe in his sixty-four-gun ship barreling after d'Estaing's ninety-gun ship had as much to do with his innate English impulse to heckle the French as it did his "energy and confidence in himself as a seaman"? Naturally, dealing with the French fleet was within Howe's job description. But before heading up the armada that would engulf New York in 1776, Admiral Howe had harbored mixed feelings about Britain's war on her colonists. As a member of Parliament, he had voted against the Coercive/"Intolerable" Acts of 1774, the retribution for the Boston Tea Party. I would imagine that chasing after Frenchmen in 1778, on the other hand, gave him no pause in any sense of the word. So Howe's spirited pursuit of the French and the patriots' overreaction to the French abandoning Newport might be related.

The Americans, who had been British for centuries and not British for only three years, were quick to turn on the French after Newport—too quick. Most of that ire can be explained by the current events in Rhode Island, but some of the patriot disdain was older, in their blood. They certainly said so.

When John Laurens wrote to his father about observing the hostility toward France spread across New England, he echoed Sullivan's language about ancient prejudices: "I saw very plainly when I was at Boston that our ancient hereditary prejudices were very far from being eradicated."

Alas, more than French feelings were hurt. In Boston, an altercation between French troops and a mob of locals "proceeded from harsh words to more dangerous blows," reported Laurens. "Two valuable French officers who attempted to quell the riot were much abused, and one of them, the Count de Sauveur it is feared will not recover." He did not.

Killing one's ally is always an awkward moment in any alliance. What made the situation with the departed Chevalier de Saint-Sauveur even more of a pickle was that his was a Catholic corpse.

In 1778, Catholicism was still illegal in Protestant Boston. France being a bulwark of Catholicism was another source of the Anglo-French feud, and Massachusetts inherited that legacy. The Boston we know as the Catholic capital of America was decades off, the product of mass immigration from Ireland during the potato famine of the 1840s. Boston was founded in 1630 by Puritans who wanted to purge the Church of England of its Catholic trappings. They also despised the actual Catholic Church of Rome so much that "Antichrist" was what Massachusetts Bay colonists called the pope.

Which explains in part why the new U.S. commissioner in France, the Puritan descendant John Adams of Massachusetts, would have such a fitful, frustrating time in Paris. Adams himself described his image among his hosts as "a Man who did not understand a Word of French—awkward in his Figure—awkward in his Dress—No Abilities—a perfect Bigot—and fanatic."

Even the prettiest thing Adams would ever write—a late-in-life appreciation of the aesthetic merits of an ice storm wrecking the fruit trees at his farm—celebrated nature's terrible beauty at the expense of his old allies. "Every tree was a chandelier of cut glass," he wrote. "I have seen a queen of France with 18 millions of livres of diamonds upon her person and I declare that all the charms of her face and figure added to all the glitter of her jewels did not make an impression on me equal to that presented by every shrub."

In order to placate Admiral D'Estaing and his troops over the slaying of the French lieutenant, the Boston fathers did offer Saint-Sauveur a proper burial, a hush-hush funeral in the middle of the night in the crypt of King's Chapel on Tremont Street. King's Chapel being the church at the burying ground where lie the city's Puritan forebears, Governor John Winthrop, of "city upon a hill" fame, and his minister John Cotton, who preached the farewell sermon when Winthrop and his shipmates departed England in 1630. I could say something about how being buried near some French papist was probably making Calvinists like Winthrop and Cotton roll over in their graves, but I believe in science.

The city promised d'Estaing it would build a monument in Saint-Sauveur's honor, which it finally got around to plopping down in front of the chapel during the later French alliance of World War I. (Fun fifteen-minute field trip: At King's Chapel, pay respects to Saint-Sauveur, Winthrop, and Cotton, remembering to glance at the other charming headstones—say what you will about Puritans, they knew how to carve a winged skull. Then mosey a few hundred feet up Tremont to Granary Burying Ground, where lie John Hancock, Paul Revere, and Samuel Adams—known to the French as "the famous Adams," grumbled his not-as-famous cousin John.)

Boston's remorse over Lieutenant Saint-Sauveur's death went a long way in patching things up with the French after Newport. Reporting to the king of France, d'Estaing described "the public and sincere marks of the regret of the Americans." At a party for the French at John Hancock's house on Beacon Hill, Hancock gave d'Estaing a portrait of George Washington as a gift. Lafayette wrote to Washington, "I never saw a man so glad at possessing his sweetheart's picture, as the admiral was to receive yours."

The alliance endured. And endured and endured. The French entrance into the war, contrary to Steuben's hunch, did not so much end the war as delay its conclusion. In Paris, John Adams wrote of foreign minister Vergennes's knack for "keep-[ing] his Hand under our Chin, to prevent Us, from drowning, but not to lift our Heads out of Water."

In November of 1778 Washington ruminated on the alliance in a letter to Henry Laurens, "Hatred to England may carry some into an excess of Confidence in France; especially when motives of gratitude are thrown into the scale." He added, "I am heartily disposed to entertain the most favourable sentiments of our new ally."

Washington would not be inaugurated for more than a decade but this letter makes clear he was not only thinking ahead; he was also already thinking like a head of state. He mulled over the unforeseen consequences of approving Lafayette's request to lead an attack on Canada for France. While Washington was not sure what a postwar Canada reoccupied by France would mean for a postwar United States, he was sure he did not want to find out.

He connected various dots—Spain's control of New Orleans, the French king's diplomatic (and familial) ties to Spain, France's more cordial history with Indian tribes. Would a Franco-Spanish-Indian confederation have the United States surrounded?

While he did not question Lafayette's motives in wanting to bring Quebec back into the French fold, Washington was suspicious of the puppet masters at Versailles. Besides, even if France conquered Canada with, he wrote, "the purest intentions, there is the greatest danger that, in the progress of the business . . . and, perhaps, urged on by the solicitations and wishes of the Canadians, she would alter her views."

Foreshadowing his later isolationism as president, Washington opined, "It is a maxim founded on the universal experience of mankind, that no nation is to be trusted farther than it is bound by its interest."

In the end, France would be too preoccupied fighting off the British in the Caribbean and India to summon the energy and resources needed to reconquer Quebec. And when France reacquired Louisiana from Spain, Napoleon promptly sold it to the administration of Thomas Jefferson for a song—that song being "Don't Fence Me In." However, the War of 1812 did confirm that Washington was dead-on about keeping an eye on those shifty Canadians.

In January of 1779, Lafayette sailed home for a yearlong visit. After a few days of house arrest (in a fancy house) as a nominal punishment for his insubordinate exit from France,

Louis XVI forgave him. "I had the honor of being consulted by all the ministers and . . . of being kissed by all the ladies," Lafayette boasted.

Once the French government turned down his request to storm Canada, he turned his attention to planning a French attack on the British homeland, a plot that also came to naught, though rumors of French invaders did put London on alert. The most concrete accomplishment of his trip home was once again knocking up his wife, who gave birth to Georges Washington Lafayette on December 24, 1779.

Lafayette made a nuisance of himself writing letters and calling upon government officials such as Foreign Minister Vergennes and Prime Minister Maurepas, lobbying for French reinforcements to be sent to his American friends. Whether or not Lafayette's efforts helped—and Franklin was also on the case—they did not hurt.

On March 5, 1780, Vergennes ordered Lafayette back to America to resume his post in the Continental Army. To that end the government had purchased a frigate, the *Hermione*, to ferry him back to the United States so as to reassure Washington that a considerable French expeditionary force would soon follow (and, one suspects, to get Lafayette out of Vergennes's hair).

On May 6, 1780, Lafayette wrote to Washington from Boston Harbor, "Here I am, my dear general . . . in the midst of the joy I feel in finding myself again one of your loving soldiers." According to Lafayette, upon the news of his return, Washington's "eyes filled with tears of joy."

On May 10 they were reunited. It was a happy occasion until Lafayette took a look around the camp. He noticed "an Army that is reduced to nothing, that wants provisions, that has not one of the necessary means to make war."

An opinion confirmed two days later when Charleston fell: General Benjamin Lincoln, a veteran of the Boston Siege and Saratoga, surrendered to British commander in chief Sir Henry Clinton, turning five thousand Continentals into prisoners of war. Already in control of Georgia, Clinton would leave Cornwallis to finish off the Carolinas, raising the question, Whither Virginia?

On July 10, 1780, the promised French fleet bearing six thousand troops commanded by Lieutenant General Jean-Baptiste Donatien de Vimeur, Comte de Rochambeau, put in at Newport, the British garrison there having decamped to smite Charleston. Good news, no doubt, though Rochambeau had to put out from France with only a fraction of his ships, troops, and supplies such as gunpowder because an enemy squadron was on his heels.

Washington dispatched Lafayette to Newport. His brother-in-law, the Viscount de Noailles, was happy to see him. Rochambeau less so. Washington had forwarded a letter confirming he trusted Lafayette as a general and friend. But before the fifty-five-year-old Rochambeau could dwell on the travesty of having to confer with some twenty-two-year-old whippersnapper, Lafayette briefed him on their bigger problems. Namely, the sorry state of Washington's army and the travesty of five thousand patriot POWs at Charleston.

ROCHAMBEAU

Naturally, Washington had assigned Lafayette to propose a collaborative attack on New York. Rochambeau said it would have to wait for the rest of his troops to arrive. Especially since a new British fleet reached New York a couple of days after the French landed at Newport. And speaking of Newport, the town that would be the French base of operations for the next year was not in move-in condition. His troops would need housing. His troops would need cheese.

Lafayette pressed Rochambeau so hard to reconsider that he would be forced to apologize for overstepping. After that, Rochambeau communicated with Washington directly and the correspondence was so cordial, they remained pen pals until Washington's death.

August brought more bad news—a message from Vergennes that Rochambeau's reinforcements were stuck at home because of a British blockade, and word of Horatio Gates's embarrassing loss at Camden, South Carolina.

On September 20, Washington took Knox, Hamilton, and Lafayette to Hartford to meet with Rochambeau and his officers, including the Swedish count rumored to be Marie Antoinette's lover, Axel von Fersen the Younger.

Fersen sized up Washington: "He is very cold, speaks little, but is courteous and frank. A shade of sadness overshadows his countenance, which is not unbecoming, and gives him an interesting air."

Washington presented an eight-page plan to—what else?—attack New York before winter. But the French, Fersen noted, "would not be rushed."

In the end, Washington agreed not to initiate a major battle unless the French held "at least temporary command of the sea along that part of the coast closest to the proposed action."

Washington was disappointed about New York, but he told Lafayette, "We must consult our means rather than our wishes." At least on his way back to White Plains he could look forward to stopping at West Point to visit his friend Benedict Arnold.

General Arnold was a no-show, and they soon discovered why. Hamilton alerted Washington that a British spy—John André, the aforementioned squatter in Franklin's Philadelphia house—had been intercepted with papers from Arnold in his boot, including damaging information about West Point's defenses and a letter about various military matters from Washington to Arnold. Washington asked to see Lafayette and Knox—Knox, who never could have made his daring journey to fetch the artillery at Ticonderoga if Arnold and Ethan Allen had not stormed that fort in '75.

"Arnold has betrayed me," Washington informed them. He wondered aloud, "Whom can we trust now?"

Answer: Franklin.

With Clinton controlling New York City, Cornwallis terrorizing the South, and the French preoccupied with sprucing up their digs in Newport, a desperate Washington contemplated another winter. In October of 1780, he wrote to Franklin, "Our present situation makes one of two things essential to us. A Peace, or the most vigorous aid of our Allies particularly in the article of money."

After all those years in France cajoling, flattering, and making nice, the last-ditch letter Franklin wrote to Vergennes was void of sweet talk. It was simple and direct and full of fear. Congress was in danger. The redcoats were on the rise. If America were to fall, a separation like its current rift with Britain "may not occur again in the Course of Ages; and that the Possession of those fertile and extensive Regions and that Vast Sea Coast, will afford them so broad a Basis for future Greatness, by the rapid Growth of their Commerce: and Breed of Seamen and Soldier, as will enable them to become the Terror of Europe."

He asked for twenty-five million livres. France kicked in six, which was six more than Washington had. This was among the happiest developments of the war (if you try not to think too hard about the guillotine).

"My knowledge of his personal courage led me to expect that he would decide to blow his brains out," Lafayette wrote of Benedict Arnold. No such luck. In fact, the newly minted British brigadier general was alive and well and commanding a Loyalist regiment in Portsmouth, Virginia. Washington ordered Lafayette to lead a division of New England and New Jersey light infantrymen to meet up with General Steuben in Virginia and, with the help of French forces sailing down from Newport, corner the traitor, then hang him.

The lack of funds made the trek south with twelve hundred men, many of them shoeless, extra arduous. Lafayette's most annoying qualities—being a single-minded suck-up prone to histrionic correspondence—made him a first-rate advocate for his men. He charmed one city after another out of food and supplies. In Philadelphia he talked the new French ambassador into springing for flour and pork and convinced a bankrupt Congress to cough up some rum money.

That I have been to Arnold's tomb in a London church is a testament to Lafayette's failure to string him up in Virginia. The crypt area of St. Mary's in Battersea currently functions as a kindergarten that keeps its fish tank next to the plaque honoring "the sometime general in the army of George Washington."

Once the Royal Navy chased off the French ships carrying the troops that were supposed to help pin down Arnold at Portsmouth, Lafayette's little division was forced to call off the manhunt. They departed Virginia and turned back around to rejoin the main army north of New York City.

In Maryland, Lafayette received new orders from Washington to trudge back to Virginia to "reinforce General Greene as speedily as possible." Greene had taken over as commander of the army's Southern Department after Horatio Gates rode north in a panic, abandoning his doomed troops in the Battle of Camden. So Lafayette's dog-eared division had to backtrack through the same mosquito-infested terrain they had just trudged through to throw in with the decimated dregs of the Continental Army in the South that Greene was trying to rebuild with Steuben's help, an especially difficult task given the forfeiture of five thousand men when Charleston surrendered. Greene described the severe deficiency of men, weapons, and supplies in the South as "totally deranged."

Worn out from the aborted mission to capture Arnold, some of Lafayette's troops deserted then and there. Exasperated and desperate for provisions, he wrote to the French ambassador such a melodramatic chronicle of his famished troops' torn-up feet and scab-covered hands that once the letter was forwarded to Vergennes, the foreign minister promptly wrote to Lafayette, "The tableau you painted of the condition of the Americans is truly distressing." He said the French government would guarantee another loan for the patriots of ten million livres from a Dutch bank.

Vergennes also informed Lafayette, "M. le Comte de Grasse, who commands our fleet in the Antilles, has been ordered to send part of his fleet to the coast of North America sometime before next winter." Not a particularly poetic sentence, and yet it is so significant it's worth rereading.

I read somewhere that Colonial Williamsburg was supposed to be "Republican Disneyland." But the actor-interpreter playing George Washington is perturbed that there aren't enough taxes, saying that if Congress had the power to tax for revenue, this war wouldn't have lasted six long years. States' rights, he says, that's the problem. A strong federal government would allow us to put behind us our local pursuits, our absurd and petty jealousies, and foster the greater good of the larger community. Then he says nice things about the French.

Not only is this fellow in the Washington getup railing

against the trouble with states' rights (and dropping the jaws of half the white guys in his audience), there is nothing remotely happiest-place-on-earth about his demeanor. In fact, my thirteen-year-old traveling companion describes this Washington as "super irritated." And he is, though not nearly as irate as the colonial shoemaker I'd met that afternoon whom I'd mistakenly called a cobbler. (A cobbler repairs! A shoemaker makes!)

The Washington reenactor introduced himself as the "commander in chief of the combined allied armies that are presently gathering in this vicinity." That would put him here in Williamsburg in September of 1781. He says Cornwallis is trapped at Yorktown thanks to "more French vessels floating at the mouth of the Chesapeake than the British have in all of North America." So he's hopeful but there's a crabby catch in his voice because he is addressing us as the citizens of Virginia. "Virginia," he says, "owes Lafayette a great debt, as he's been defending you for months."

General Anthony Wayne's brigade of barefoot Pennsylvanians has marched down to help us, and apparently we Virginians cannot be bothered to scrounge them up some shoes. Thinking back to my altercation with the non-cobbler nearby, I resist the urge to raise my hand and utter the four most reassuring words in the English language: *I know a guy.*

This is my first time to Colonial Williamsburg, and I had worried that it would be too chipper, too reassuring, an infomercial for the preindustrial good olde days that Frank Lloyd Wright once denounced for its "mawkish sentimentality." But within the first hour of our arrival, my family and I fall in with an angry mob. If they are sentimental, it is only because they're nostalgic for a time the government of Great Britain respected their constitutional rights as Englishmen.

They are storming the royal governor's palace. It is April 20, 1775. Unbeknownst to them, the first shot at Lexington had been fired the day before. Patrick Henry had given a speech that alarmed Governor Dunmore. Dunmore—"that Scottish wretch!"—had ordered Royal Navy sailors to steal the town militia's gunpowder supply in the middle of the night, and boy were they peeved.

Someone calls out, "The whole reason Virginia exists is to expand the British Empire." I look around at the backdrop of restored or re-created red brick buildings—Georgian buildings, in the symmetrical style in fashion between the reigns of George III and his great-grandfather George I. When we got here, my sister said that Colonial Williamsburg "looks so foreign." She meant that it looks like England, not America. And that is our angry mob's point. The reason they are angry is because they're British and they're just supposed to put up with being treated like they're Irish?

Robbed of gunpowder, their only available weapon is sarcasm. "I'm more British than some miserable wretch walking up the street in London and sitting in Parliament!" one of them yells.

These actors in period garb are not the upbeat butter churners I had dreaded. They are livid and loud. I am enjoying it. My sister is enjoying it. But then I look over at my nephew, Owen, wearing a Continental hunting tunic and tricornered hat and holding the wooden musket he had just picked out at Colonial Williamsburg's costume rental shop. He is trying to blend in amongst the reenactors, joining their chant. "Liberty or death!" they holler. "Liberty or death!" Who better to identify with surly victims of tyranny raging against their oppressors than a teenager on a car trip with his aunt and mom?

Colonial Williamsburg could stage another reenactment composed entirely of readings from the morose letters exchanged among the leadership of the Continental Army in 1781 about the uphill task of defending Virginia without much help from actual Virginians. Greene informed Steuben, "The state is lifeless and inactive unless they are often electrified."

After only five of the five hundred recruits the state government promised him bothered to report for duty, Steuben confessed to Greene, "I am not less tired of this state than they are of me."

Lafayette wrote to Alexander Hamilton from Richmond that Cornwallis had him outnumbered five to one. Lafayette said he was waiting around for General Wayne to show up with his Pennsylvanians so that he "may at least be beat with some decency."

Thomas Jefferson was Virginia's governor. When Lafayette complained to him about the state's lack of militia, food, horses, weapons, and just general dearth of military hustle, Jefferson agreed with him, admitting, "Mild Laws, a People not used to prompt obedience, a want of provisions of War & means of procuring them render our orders often ineffectual."

Jefferson's big accomplishment of 1781, aside from eluding

the redcoats sent to Monticello to kidnap him, was writing the first draft of *Notes on the State of Virginia*. The book hints at the swooping magnitude of Jefferson's mind, recording what he was thinking about architecture, Indians, farmers, slavery, other people's gods, the Blue Ridge Mountains, the Shenandoah and the Potomac and "the moment of their junction," how Virginia was "worth a voyage across the Atlantic" to behold. Basically, the governor of Virginia had thoughts on everything but how to arm and feed and reinforce the soldiers risking their lives to save his state.

In a desperate attempt to convince the state assembly to procure the Continentals some badly needed horses, Nathanael Greene wrote to Jefferson in April, "It is in vain to expect protection from an Army which is not supported."

Virginia's "government wants energy" was how Lafayette described Jefferson's administration to Hamilton. "Militia are not numerous, without arms, and not used to war." Adding to the deficit of material aid, Lafayette pointed out he was short on information: "There are accounts that Lord Cornwallis is very strong; others make him very weak. In this country there is no getting good intelligence."

Forced to organize his own spy network, Lafayette recruited James, a slave from New Kent County. James pretended to be a runaway, volunteering as a servant and guide to Benedict Arnold, then Cornwallis, passing along intelligence about British troop movements to Lafayette. After the war, James successfully petitioned the Virginia Assembly for his freedom and a war pension, using a letter of recommendation from Lafayette

CORNWALLIS

to make his case. James took the last name of Lafayette in honor of his former commanding officer.

By May of 1781, Benedict Arnold had returned to New York, and Cornwallis took charge in Virginia. Lafayette's assignment from Washington was to avoid a full-scale confrontation. "No rational person will condemn you for not fighting with the odds against you and while so much is depending on it," wrote Washington. The goal was to keep Cornwallis flustered and tired while sidestepping the full force of Britain's wrath.

Though avoiding warfare was never Lafayette's first impulse, he reassured Washington, "Were I to fight a battle, I should be cut to pieces, the militia dispersed and the arms lost." He vowed instead "to skirmish, but not to engage too far . . . I am not strong enough even to get beaten."

With the arrival of Wayne in June and the addition of militia rounded up by Steuben, Lafayette ended up with nearly four thousand men. As Cornwallis ripped his way across Virginia, occupying Richmond and then Williamsburg, Lafayette was always on his tail, dispatching small parties of riflemen to snipe at the army's periphery, dropping a handful of redcoats a pop, keeping them perpetually on guard, on edge, and on the move. In a letter to Clinton snatched by the patriots, Cornwallis promised to capture Lafayette. "The boy cannot escape me," he vowed.

Celebrating the Fourth of July outside of Williamsburg, Lafayette crowed to Washington that the men he commanded were "far superior to any British troops . . . their presence here, I must confess, has saved this State."

One of Lafayette's aides, James McHenry, confided in a letter to Nathanael Greene that he worried about Lafayette and "Mad Anthony" Wayne egging each other on. "Wayne was impetuous," he wrote, "and the Marquis loved glory." McHenry feared that between the two of them, "military ardor should be too powerful for reason." Greene advised McHenry to try to keep Lafayette in check: "You are useful to him in moderating his military ardor, which no doubt is heated by the fire of [Wayne] . . . who by the by is an excellent officer."

On July 6 Cornwallis set a trap, and Lafayette and Wayne got caught in it. When the redcoats crossed the James River near Jamestown on their way to Portsmouth, Cornwallis tricked Lafayette into believing that most of the army had gone on ahead, leaving only a weak rear guard that would be an easy target for the patriots to polish off. Lafayette took the bait, dispatching an advance guard commanded by Wayne to pounce on the stragglers near Green Spring plantation—only to find Cornwallis's entire army roaring back at them. According to Wayne, the sudden appearance of seven thousand British regulars presented him with "a choice of difficulties." Wayne decided against a retreat and ordered its opposite—a bayonet charge against the Brits' front line. Lafayette, watching nearby, immediately understood his mistake and galloped toward the fray. He personally led a Continental counterattack on Cornwallis to cover Wayne's troops backing out, though twenty-eight of his Pennsylvanians were killed. Lafayette and Wayne's shared knack for quick thinking and stupid bravery turned around a potential catastrophe. Because Cornwallis continued on to Portsmouth, Lafayette painted the Battle of Green Spring as a patriot victory rather than a mishap that could have been worse. In a letter to Greene, Lafayette admitted, "There were serious blunders on both sides," adding that at least the appearance of a British retreat "will look good in a gazette."

Henry Clinton, failing to see the value in Cornwallis's "unmeaning and unprofitable ramble through Virginia," ordered him to return his troops to New York in case Washington and Rochambeau were up to something. Considering these would be the same troops who would soon be surrendering to Washington and Rochambeau, sending them north was not a terrible idea. Clinton, however, changed his mind and redirected Cornwallis and his army to proceed first to the Chesapeake Bay to build a fortified naval base at one of the harbors there. Cornwallis kept Lafayette busy the next few weeks skulking behind him as he tooled around coastal Virginia picking a spot. As the actor playing Washington at Colonial Williamsburg explained it, "Cornwallis did not make a mistake. We turned what he had done into a mistake."

Back in May, Washington recorded in his diary that he had met with Rochambeau in Connecticut, where they began making tentative plans "to commence an operation against New York." However, although in his report to Admiral de Grasse, Rochambeau included New York as an option for the impending joint operation, behind Washington's back, Rochambeau nudged de Grasse toward the southern option. "The south-westerly winds and the state of defense in Virginia will probably make you prefer the Chesapeake Bay," he opined, "and it will be there that we think you may be able to render the greatest service."

On July 6, more than four thousand forces of the French Royal Army arrived from Rhode Island at Washington's camp on the Hudson, poised to help the Americans invade some still-to-be-determined British stronghold.

As if stepping out of a Tchaikovsky ballet directed by Wes Anderson, the French soldiers wore plumed black hats and white on white, brightening their snowy leggings and jackets with pops of color on their lapels—their sometimes pink lapels. As opposed to their earthier allies, who were dressed, if they were dressed, in ripped and rotting homespun like zombie Tom Joads. Baron Ludwig von Closen, one of Rochambeau's staff officers, pitied the Continentals: "It is really painful to see these brave men, almost naked."

One of the French officers was horrified that at a dinner in Washington's tent, His Excellency served the meal not in a succession of courses like in civilization. Apparently Washington "gave, on the same plate, meat, vegetables, and salad." On the *same plate*? Were these Americans people or animals?

The French soldiers' depth of training and experience, their access to good equipment, as well as their being used to such a high quality of life that they not only expected food every day, they expected foods plural served on plural plates, made them oddly appreciative of their rustic patriot cronies. After a few redcoats fired on a Franco-American team doing recon, one of Rochambeau's aides marveled, "I cannot insist too strongly how

I was surprised by the American Army. It is truly incredible that troops almost naked, poorly paid, and composed of old men and children and Negroes should behave so well on the march and under fire."

One of the French government's smarter moves was to order Rochambeau to report to Washington even though Rochambeau commanded more troops and had four decades of experience and the highest rank in the French army. For that reason, Rochambeau humored Washington's designs on New York, accompanying him to the northern tip of Manhattan to sketch out a possible strike.

In the choice of New York or Virginia, however, both generals would ultimately have to defer to Admiral de Grasse. He controlled his ships and helping out the Continentals was a distraction from defending France's lucrative sugar islands in the Caribbean. As Andrew O'Shaughnessy told me, "The French put particular stress on the Caribbean. They had Saint-Domingue—modern Haiti—which at the time was producing more sugar than anywhere else in the world. There was a real premium on sugar. It had become part of the regular diet of most people. It was hugely profitable."

On August 14, Washington received news from de Grasse that the French fleet would arrive at the Chesapeake Bay by September 3. Virginia it would be.

While Washington mourned his now-dead dream of taking back Manhattan, he quickly got on with the business of figuring out how to transport thousands of men 450 miles in six weeks.

Washington wrote to Robert Morris, the Congress's super-

De GRASSE

intendent of finance, pleading for one month's pay for his troops—in coin, not the worthless Continental paper currency. He explained, "The service they are going upon is disagreeable to the Northern regiments" and "part of the troops have not been paid anything for a long time." In the end, Washington had to borrow the money from Rochambeau, who generously offered Washington half his supply of gold Spanish coins. There is no way to overstate how this gesture endeared the French to the patriot troops. Joseph Plumb Martin, the young man who paid his last few pence for a sip of water at Valley Forge, recalled, "We each of us received a MONTH'S PAY . . . This was the first that could be called money, which we had received as wages since the year '76, or that we ever did receive till the close of the war, or indeed, ever after, as wages."

On August 17, Washington heard from Lafayette that Cornwallis had hunkered down at Yorktown. I would like to think Washington laughed. He knew the place, an old tobacco port on the Virginia Peninsula, a finger of land between the York River and the James, both of which empty into the Chesapeake Bay. When Thomas Nelson, Yorktown native and signer of the Declaration of Independence, suggested to Washington that the Continentals build a fort there back in 1777, Washington rejected the proposal. Yorktown, he informed Nelson, "by being upon a narrow neck of land would be in danger of being cut off. The enemy might very easily throw up a few ships into York and James's river . . . and land a body of men there, who by throwing up a few redoubts would intercept their retreat and oblige them to surrender."

Two things: Washington's 1777 assessment of Yorktown and being cut off and the bit about redoubts was *exactly* what was about to happen to Cornwallis in 1781. And just to make Thomas Nelson feel like even more of a jerk, Cornwallis had just commandeered Nelson's Yorktown house as his headquarters. Cornwallis was probably sleeping in Nelson's bed.

Washington ordered Lafayette to make sure to keep Cornwallis hemmed in. So as the British got on with fortifying the town, Lafayette encircled them with artillery. As the de facto Continental advance man, he also started hitting up regional governments for reinforcements and supplies. He asked Virginia to share its stores of beef, corn, and flour, and they were pretty Virginian about it. Luckily Washington and Rochambeau persuaded Admiral de Barras to sail his small French fleet down from Newport loaded with salt beef and siege guns.

On August 17, the first Continental forces crossed the Hudson en route to Yorktown, followed soon thereafter by French artillery and infantry.

Washington left some men and scores of empty tents near New York City to keep up the ruse that that was still the intended target. This con was helped along because the British had intercepted a letter from Washington to Lafayette and Greene with details about the upcoming Franco-American attack on Manhattan. Unfortunately for Henry Clinton, the letter was written before de Grasse made a beeline for the Chesapeake, and Washington had to scrap New York.

The French dandies caused a stir marching through Philadelphia September 3. The Marquis de Chastellux called their time there "a triumph." Another officer boasted that the sharp-dressed foreigners "struck with astonishment the beauties of the city." Rochambeau's chaplain got a kick out of watching the townspeople and Continentals addressing a French army messenger as a general: "His embroidered [jacket], his tunic with silver fringe, his emblazoned headdress, his cane with its golden knob, were the sources of this mistake. Each time that he approached his master to get orders they thought that he was giving them."

Returning from a boat excursion to check out the Delaware River forts, Rochambeau was startled to see "General Washington waving his hat at me with demonstrative gestures of the greatest joy." As if that wasn't out of character enough, Washington then gave Rochambeau a hug, telling him the news that Admiral de Grasse was already in the Chesapeake, along with twenty-eight large warships and a slew of smaller support vessels carrying more than three thousand ground troops. With the men already onshore backing up Lafayette and the French ships in the harbor, they had Cornwallis surrounded. "I never saw a man more thoroughly and openly delighted than was General Washington at this moment," recalled the Duc de Lauzun.

De Grasse was in the Chesapeake but the Caribbean was on his mind. On September 4, he tried to coax Lafayette into an immediate assault on Cornwallis just to get it over with. This was contrary to Washington's orders, which were to keep Cornwallis from escaping and wait for the allied army to arrive so they could all gang up on him together. De Grasse cajoled Lafayette by promising "to further your glory." Lafayette later confessed, "The temptation was great, but even if the attack had succeeded, it would necessarily have cost a great deal of blood." Therefore he decided "not to sacrifice the soldiers entrusted to me to personal ambition." Lafayette was growing up. Two days later he turned twenty-four.

Meanwhile, en route to the Chesapeake, Washington stopped at Mount Vernon. He had not been home for six years. When he departed for Philadelphia in 1775, the Congress appointed him commander in chief and he rode straight to the siege of Boston, then from there to New York, then Trenton, Brandy-wine, Germantown, Valley Forge, and so on. Through it all, his homesickness was a source of both distraction and strength. In a letter to his cousin and Mount Vernon's manager, Lund Washington, in September of 1776, Washington wallowed in the indignities of the debacle in New York: "I tell you that I never was in such an unhappy, divided state since I was born." Then he sought comfort in cheerier subjects: "With respect to the chimney . . ." He wrote that letter a month after throw-ing up his hands at Kips Bay in Manhattan, wondering if the fleeing quitters around him were the men with whom he was being asked to defend America. Imagining specific, attainable improvements to his Virginia house must have been a solace, a fantasy of comfort and control: "The chimney in the new room should be exactly in the middle of it—the doors and every thing else to be exactly answerable and uniform—in short I would have the whole executed in a masterly manner."

Washington's love of Mount Vernon had a profound impact on the character of the future republic. At war's end, when an

American painter explained to the monarch of Great Britain that rather than stay on as dictator or king, Washington planned to retire and return to his life as a farmer, George III remarked, "If he does that, he will be the greatest man in the world."

Washington repeated this performance as president, leaving office after two terms rather than staying on as president for life, because he honestly wanted to live out his days, as Voltaire put it, cultivating his own garden—and painting his dining room the world's most alarming shade of green.

Washington's homebody side tempered his ambition, staving off the lure of power. Compare Mount Vernon to the abode of his closest counterpart, Napoleon Bonaparte, whose house outside Paris, Malmaison, is full of tented rooms meant to evoke the tents the soldier lived in on his military campaigns. If Malmaison's walls could talk, they would say, *I'd rather be anywhere else, conquering it.* Napoleon lived as he governed—like a general barking orders at the citizens of the French "republic." Forced into exile and introspection on Elba, Napoleon finally figured out, "They wanted me to be another Washington."

Washington returning to Mount Vernon in September of 1781 after six years away was a premonition that the war would end. Riding ahead of his French cohorts gave him a little time to catch up with his family (and his slaves). Rochambeau and his officers arrived the next day. The Marquis de Chastellux found the house "simple" and Martha Washington "somewhat fat, but fresh and with a pleasant face." On September 11, the anniversary of his defeat at Brandywine, Washington hosted a jolly dinner for the French. One of his aides, Jonathan Trumbull of Connecticut, was wowed by "the "great appearance of opulence and real exhibitions of hospitality and princely entertainment."

Resuming their trek to Yorktown the next morning, they bumped into a messenger with harrowing news. On September 5, a British fleet commanded by Vice Admiral Thomas Graves arrived in the Chesapeake from New York to aid Cornwallis. To avoid being trapped in the bay, Admiral de Grasse took off from Yorktown toward the open sea to confront the enemy.

There had been no news for days. Wherever the ships were, the fleet that prevailed and returned to control the mouth of the York River would control the fate of Cornwallis and ultimately the war itself. For that reason, some scholars consider this somewhat forgotten maritime dustup—referred to as the Battle of the Chesapeake or the Battle of the Virginia Capes or the plain old Battle of the Capes—to be the most important altercation of the American Revolution, a take that's all the more astonishing considering not a single American took part in it. Nor did a single American even witness it once de Grasse's ships followed Graves over the horizon.

Graves had nineteen ships of the line, compared with de Grasse's twenty-four. The reason these big battleships were called that was because that is literally how naval engagements using them were fought—in two parallel lines. Their guns could fire only straight ahead, and squeezing into a row also prevented friendly fire accidents.

If the idea of a pair of enemies politely lining up across from one another in the middle of an ocean in an orderly fashion sounds quaint, it was. Or as quaint as possible for opposing vessels with up to a hundred cannons concurrently raining hell upon each other in the inherently fearsome Atlantic.

The stiff format had some wiggle room allowing for individual initiative, human error, currents, weather, or all of the above. Graves, for instance, formed his line at an odd angle, decreasing the potency of his guns. He also failed to line up his most powerful vessels with their scariest French counterparts, pitting some of the scrawnier British ships against de Grasse's biggest. Still, after a couple of hours of nonstop shelling, there was no clear winner, though the French had been especially effective at ripping into the Brits' sails and masts. The two sides bobbed along in a stalemate until September 9, when the second French fleet, commanded by Admiral de Barras, was spotted coming down from Newport en route to Yorktown. De Grasse peeled off to join them, and on September 12 returned to port, where they had Cornwallis overwhelmingly, definitively trapped. Admiral Graves, on the other hand, hobbled on back to New York, and that's when Henry Clinton's heartaches began.

"De Grasse should be given much greater billing," Andrew O'Shaughnessy told me about the admiral's place in American history. "De Grasse took a huge risk. Rather than split his fleet and send some of the ships back to convoy French goods to France, rather than leaving ships to protect the French islands, he took every ship with him. It's often credited to Rochambeau, but de Grasse had suggested to Rochambeau that they liaise at the Chesapeake instead of attacking the British in New York, where the main army was based, that they attempt to cut off

Cornwallis. That was not Washington's plan originally; in fact, he resisted it for a while, and it was the French who persuaded him to adopt it. The reason it gets downplayed, not only is it foreign, but it's also because many people don't appreciate the naval aspect of the war and how important naval events were to the outcome. The British commander in chief had always recognized that the moment a superior French fleet arrived off the coast of America, Britain was doomed, because it could cut off any army. Which could then be surrounded by land troops. This is essentially what happened to Cornwallis. So the French victory at Chesapeake Capes was key to the victory at Yorktown. There were more French people present at Yorktown than Americans."

Colonial Williamsburg does not shy away from the French contribution to American independence. In the Q&A with George Washington, for instance, the Washington sang the praises of Admiral de Grasse, Rochambeau, Lafayette, and the French engineers, "the most able engineers in the world." (French engineering being a particular blessing during the siege of Yorktown.)

At the end of my visit, I went to Williamsburg's Market Square to watch a performance called *On to Yorktown and Victory: The General Reviews the Troops,* a military presentation set on September 28, 1781, featuring Washington and Lafayette, a nod to their reunion before Yorktown. (When Washington arrived on September 14, Lafayette was waiting for him. A Virginia militiaman reported that Lafayette "caught the General round his body, hugged him as close as it was possible, and absolutely kissed him from ear to ear once or twice . . . with as much ardor as ever an absent lover kissed his mistress on his return.")

The Lafayette reenactor, decked out in a buff and blue uniform, rode a white horse with impeccable posture and made a speech to the troops and assembled citizens. He uttered some pleasantries about the certainty of victory, acknowledged that the people and the soldiers were tired of war, and pointed toward the royal governor's palace and said that the last royal governor would be the last royal governor. Then he said, "But you could not win this war alone. You would not win this war alone. You would need help from somewhere and somehow." It was loud and clear and immaculately enunciated. And it was the truth.

I had spoken to the actor, Mark Schneider, that afternoon in Colonial Williamsburg's research library. I was taken aback when he showed up for our talk wearing the full Lafayette getup. He was simply squeezing me in between performances, but I couldn't shake the feeling that I was hallucinating or having another one of those dreams about having lunch with Puritan theologians or John Wilkes Booth.

Having portrayed Lafayette since 1999, Schneider knows his stuff. A veteran U.S. Army cavalry scout who served in Bosnia in the 1990s, he speaks of Lafayette with humor, affection, and respect, and embodies him with so much panache that I wasn't surprised to find a Facebook fan page devoted to him on the Internet—one he has nothing to do with—in which his devotees post videos of him on horseback.

What I really wanted to ask him about was what it was like

portraying Lafayette circa 2003, when France refused to back an American resolution for military action against Iraq in the United Nations Security Council, inspiring an anti-French backlash most famously and stupidly symbolized by congressional cafeterias changing the name of French fries to freedom fries.

It's how I originally got onto the topic of Lafayette in the first place. Representative Ginny Brown-Waite of Florida sponsored a bill called the American Heroes Repatriation Act of 2003. Intended to finance digging up the remains of U.S. war casualties buried in French cemeteries and reinterring them over here, the bill went nowhere. "The remains of our brave servicemen should be buried in patriotic soil, not in a country that has turned its back on the United States and on the memory of Americans who fought and died there," Brown-Waite told the *New York Times*. "It's almost as if the French have forgotten what those thousands of white crosses at Normandy represent."

Not long after reading that, I happened to be in the Berkshire Mountains to attend a wedding and stopped in at Arrowhead, the house where Herman Melville wrote *Moby-Dick*. I was struck by a tiny silk dress in a glass display case, said to be what Melville's wife, Elizabeth Knapp Shaw Melville, was wearing as a two-year-old in 1824 when she was presented to the Marquis de Lafayette on his visit to Boston. That was when I started researching Lafayette's return to America. If the French had forgotten America's help in World War II—and they had not; they just opposed a preemptive war in the Middle East based on faulty intelligence that most Americans would end up regretting anyway—it seemed obvious that Americans had forgotten France's help in our war for independence in general and the national obsession with Lafayette in particular. A fixation symbolized by a family hanging on to a little girl's dress for generations because she was wearing it when she met him, an event Elizabeth Melville herself probably had no memory of.

Mark Schneider recalled portraying Lafayette in the freedom fries era: "Well, I would say it was more of a challenge to tell the story, to talk about French help [during the revolution]. Quite often from my guests I would get, 'Hey, I wish they would help now!' or something to that effect. But telling the story, the truth speaks for itself. One of the greatest compliments I've ever received portraying Lafayette was from an older gentleman who listened to the story of Lafayette, with me telling the personal sacrifice that he made and then the sacrifice France made by getting involved in this war and helping us win independence. It brought him to tears, and he said at the end, 'You know, I hated the French until I came in this room. Thank you for sharing that story. I needed to hear that story. I no longer feel that way about the French. Thank you for telling me the truth and the facts about this. Now maybe I'll reevaluate my opinions on the French.' I had accomplished my goal, and that was to tell the true story of the American Revolution and the sacrifice that so many people made—the people here in America, but also those that helped us."

The next morning, my relatives and I went to Yorktown for the anniversary festivities. "Happy Yorktown Day!" hollered the ladies from the Comte de Grasse Chapter of the Daughters of the American Revolution marching in the annual parade. At the memorial ceremony put on by the town, after the French national anthem was sung, General Jean-Paul Paloméros, a French commander at NATO, spoke of America's enthusiasm over the return of Lafayette in 1824 and expressed his country's gratitude "to the Americans who twice traveled across the ocean to fight a world's war." Over at the battlefield, we drove from the site of the French encampment to the French artillery park to the French Cemetery, where someone had left a single yellow daisy on the plaque commemorating the burial of fifty unknown French soldiers. Then we went for lunch on the York River waterfront at the Water Street Grille, a few yards away from a statue of Admiral de Grasse. There were freedom fries on the menu.

On September 17, 1781, a few days before the allied army surrounded Yorktown, Cornwallis wrote to his commander in chief Henry Clinton in New York, "This place is in no state of defense. If you cannot relieve me very soon, you must be prepared to hear the Worst."

At the end of the month, Cornwallis abandoned his newly built outer defenses to crouch his troops close to the river, where he hoped to be rescued by a British fleet that would somehow also fight off Admiral de Grasse.

Clinton replied to Cornwallis, "Your Lordship may be as-

sured that I am doing every thing in my power to relieve you."
Mentioning that Admiral Graves was busy repairing his fleet
(after the damage suffered in the Battle of the Capes), Clinton
comforted Cornwallis that they would depart New York Harbor as soon as possible "if the winds permit, and no unforeseen
accident happens." Though Clinton added ominously, "This,
however, is subject to disappointment."

The lesson of Yorktown is the value of cooperation—the lack
of it among Britain's top commanders, and the overwhelming strength of the Franco-American alliance. Nine thousand
American regulars and militia, nine thousand French land
forces, and a whopping twenty-eight thousand Frenchmen serving on board the fleets of de Grasse and Barras in the Chesapeake were always going to defeat Cornwallis's eight thousand
troops if the British fleet failed to show.

A more interesting aspect of the Franco-American collaboration was the way the French and American officers kept talking
each other out of bad ideas. Just as Admiral de Grasse cornered
Washington into exchanging his reckless obsession with retak-
ing New York City for the more attainable goal of ensnaring
Cornwallis in the Chesapeake, Washington and Rochambeau
convinced Admiral de Grasse to stay the course after the Battle
of the Capes, pressing him to extend his self-imposed deadline
of returning to the Caribbean by October 15.

At the end of September, Washington passed along to de
Grasse what he considered routine intel about rumors of a new
British fleet with an unknown quantity of ships, perhaps three
to ten, having arrived in New York, presumably intending to

head south to help Cornwallis. Alarmed, de Grasse replied to Washington, "The enemy are beginning to be almost equal to us"—a blatant falsehood—"and it would be imprudent of me to put myself in a position where I could not engage them in battle." De Grasse concluded, "I shall set sail as soon as the wind permits me."

Washington's response to receiving such worrisome news was to politely explain to de Grasse how this update filled him with "painful anxiety."

In his diary, Rochambeau's officer Closen complained that these "turbulent men of the sea . . . think of nothing but cruising, with no desire to cooperate with the land forces."

Because de Grasse's ships were keeping Cornwallis from making a break for it and guarding against a possible British rescue operation, because the outcome of the entire operation and therefore the outcome of the war depended on Cornwallis looking out at the water and seeing dozens of French battleships staring back at him, Washington beseeched the admiral, "If you withdraw your maritime force from the position agreed upon . . . that no future day can restore to us a similar occasion for striking a decisive blow."

Washington dispatched Lafayette and Closen to de Grasse's flagship, the *Ville de Paris*, anchored at the mouth of the York River. Lafayette was to hand de Grasse Washington's letter and give the admiral the hard sell about remaining in the Chesapeake. By the time they arrived, de Grasse's own captains had already voted against leaving. De Grasse agreed to stay. Prompting such a gale-force sigh of relief from Washington, it's a wonder the fleet wasn't blown back to Bermuda.

Sir Henry Clinton—and by extension Cornwallis—was no less beholden to the "turbulent men of the sea" than his fellow landlubbers Washington and Rochambeau. After the war, Clinton would end up taking all the blame for dithering in New York instead of hastening to save Cornwallis; his reputation would never recover. Yet Admiral Graves should share some of the blame. The diary of a forty-year veteran, Captain Frederick Mackenzie, one of Clinton's adjutants in New York, estimated that repairs to Graves's ships would not be completed until October 10. Then, he figured, it would take three days for all the ships to clear the bar of New York Harbor and another seven for them to make it to Virginia. Mackenzie's predictions were close. Clinton and Graves did not arrive in the Chesapeake until October 24, unaware that Cornwallis had already surrendered on the 19th.

In the meantime, Washington kept on beefing up his team. He implored Virginia's new governor, his old friend Thomas Nelson of Yorktown, "that every exertion may be made to feed and supply our army while we have occasion to continue in the State." Unlike his brainier predecessor—former governor Jefferson had happily "retired to my farm, my family and books from which I think nothing will evermore separate me"—Nelson called for "vigorous exertions" by the people of Virginia to scare up food, supplies, and transport for the incoming armies. Nelson also called upon militiamen to head to Yorktown "with a gun of any sort," and ended up personally leading three thousand Virginians in the siege that damaged his own home. There were even tall tales about Nelson offering a cash reward to the first artillery team to successfully shell his house.

With Nelson leading the militia, Washington assigned Generals Lafayette, Steuben, and Benjamin Lincoln to lead the three divisions of Continental regulars. Lincoln was officially Washington's number two, having been with the Continentals since the siege of Boston, serving in the New York campaign and at Saratoga before his career low of surrendering Charleston to Henry Clinton.

Lafayette divided up the command of his two brigades between his friends and fellow members of Washington's military family, Alexander Hamilton and John Laurens. (Laurens's father, Congressman Henry Laurens, was at that moment imprisoned as a traitor in the Tower of London. The British captured his ship when he was en route to the Netherlands to negotiate an agreement with the Dutch. After the surrender, Lafayette would help broker the prisoner exchange that traded Laurens for the Americans' new POW, Cornwallis.)

On October 3, Dr. James Thacher, a surgeon with the Sixteenth Massachusetts Regiment, recorded in his diary one of the more sickening consequences of how the arrival of the allies on the outskirts of Yorktown had blocked the redcoats from foraging in the countryside for food—for themselves and their animals. The British, preparing to withstand the coming siege, were "killing off their horses in great numbers; six or seven hundred of these valuable animals have been killed, and their carcases are almost continually floating down the river." If the thought of looking at a river clogged with six hundred horse corpses sounds repugnant, consider the smell.

On October 6, Washington wrote to the Congress, "We shall this night open trenches."

The besiegers would encircle the besieged with a series of parallel trenches, choking them with each advance. Hence the real heroes of Yorktown were the Corps of Sappers and Miners, the men who dug the ditches laid out by the French engineers. (The commander of the Continental Army's Corps of Engineers, Louis Duportail, was also French, having been recruited by Franklin in 1777.) The first siege line would be roughly two miles long, positioned about six hundred yards from the outermost British fortifications.

According to Joseph Plumb Martin, who had joined the Sappers and Miners as a sergeant the year before, "We now began to make preparations for laying close siege to the enemy. We had holed him and nothing remained but to dig him out."

In a ranger talk out on the battlefield, Linda Williams of the National Park Service walked us through the siege. She said, "If you have fifteen hundred French and American soldiers with picks and shovels digging and three thousand soldiers keeping an eye out while they're digging, you're going to be making some noise. They wanted to dig the first siege line without the British knowing they're out here."

She continued, "On October the 5th it began to rain heavily, and it continued to rain into the night of October the 6th. And what that rain did—first, the clouds covered the moon; second, the rain made the ground a little easier to dig; and third, the rain softened the ground and helped mute the sound of all those tools. So the night of October 6 they snuck up and they started digging. I'm sure they were scared. They completed it in one night, and the British didn't know they were out there. So when the British looked out at first light and saw the siege line upon them, they must have done some sort of collective gulp."

Once the trench was completed, the allies let rip their artillery. Sergeant Martin recalled that the signal for commencing to fire was the raising of an American flag and that his pride swelled when he saw it "waving majestically in the very faces of our implacable adversaries . . . A simultaneous discharge of all the guns in the line followed; the French troops accompanying it with 'Huzza for the Americans!'"

Cornwallis wrote to Clinton, "On the evening of the 9th their batteries opened, and have since continued firing without intermission."

According to Ranger Williams, "It was going to be an intense, nonstop bombardment, averaging seventeen hundred cannonballs and mortar shells a day. They said the peninsula was shaking as if from thunderbolts. One American officer described how at night you could see the mortar shells raining down on Yorktown with the fuses shooting off sparks. He described them as falling comets."

According to the Marquis de Chastellux, Henry Knox

"scarcely ever quitted the batteries." The French officer admired "the extraordinary progress of the American artillery, as well as the capacity and knowledge of a great many officers employed in it."

Dr. Thacher wrote in his journal, "I have more than once witnessed fragments of the mangled bodies and limbs of the British soldiers thrown into the air by the bursting of our shells."

Cornwallis warned Clinton, "Against so powerful an attack we cannot hope to make a very long resistance."

On October 11, Sergeant Martin of the Sappers and Miners wrote, "We now began our second parallel, about half way between our works and theirs. There were two strong redoubts held by the British, on their left."

"A redoubt is a heavily defended earthen fort," said Ranger Williams. Pointing toward the river at "that mound of earth with stakes coming out of it," she told us, "That is Redoubt Number 9, and beyond those large oaks, there's Redoubt Number 10. It was necessary for us to possess those redoubts before we could complete our trenches. The British soldiers defending those were hard-core. The Americans and the French had to capture them. So the night of October 14th, four hundred French troops were going to try to overwhelm Redoubt Number 9, and four hundred Americans were going to try to overwhelm Redoubt Number 10. And the Americans were told they were going to attack this heavily defended position with unloaded muskets, just with their fixed bayonets. It was a nighttime attack and they didn't want to be shooting each other. They were commanded by that gentleman on your ten-dollar bill, Alexander Hamilton, the future secretary of the Treasury."

Originally, Lafayette had assigned his fellow Frenchman, longtime aide, and *Victory* shipmate Lieutenant Colonel Jean-Joseph de Gimat to lead the infantry's bayonet charge on Redoubt 10. Hamilton, aware the war was winding down and that this was likely his last shot at glory, went over Lafayette's head and appealed to Washington, who overruled Lafayette and allowed Hamilton to lead.

The signal to begin the attack was "Rochambeau," which Sergeant Martin considered "a good watchword, for being pronounced Ro-sham-bow, it sounded, when pronounced quick, like rush-on-boys."

Afterward, describing his division's accomplishments to Washington, Lafayette commended "Colonel Hamilton, whose well known talents and gallantry were on this occasion most conspicuous and serviceable." He wrote, "Our obligations to him, to Colonel Gimat, to Colonel Laurens, and to each and all the officers and men, are above expression. Not one gun was fired . . . and, owing to the conduct of the commanders and the bravery of the men, the redoubt was stormed with uncommon rapidity."

It was over in five minutes. Nine Americans were killed, and Gimat, hit in the foot, was among the twenty-five who were wounded. With only sixty men to hold off four hundred Americans, the British commander of the redoubt, a Major Campbell, surrendered to Laurens. Afterward, when an unhinged captain from New Hampshire threatened Campbell with his bayonet, Hamilton stepped between them, because rules were rules.

Lafayette was down in the trench when he got word of Campbell's surrender. Admitting that it gave him "unspeakable satisfaction," he sent a note over to Baron de Viomenil, his condescending French counterpart (and Rochambeau's second in command), explaining that the Americans had already taken Redoubt 10 and did the French need any help with Redoubt 9?

"Now the French had a much harder time capturing Redoubt 9," explained Ranger Williams. "They took loaded muskets and they paid a heavy price. They had a hard time getting through, and they were accidentally shooting some of their own. They had a lot more casualties, but they finally captured Redoubt 9 in thirty minutes."

On October 15, a glum Cornwallis wrote to Clinton, who was still in New York, "Last evening the enemy carried my two advanced redoubts in the left by storm . . . My situation now becomes very critical . . . The safety of the place is, therefore, so precarious, that I cannot recommend that the fleet and army should run great risk in endeavoring to save us."

"So now Cornwallis is pretty much surrounded," said Ranger Williams. Planning to leave behind in Yorktown hundreds of ill, bedridden men, "he was going to try and take his troops who were able by boat and get them across the York River where it narrows to join the thousand he already had there at Gloucester Point." (Nowadays there's a bridge.) Washington did have a few troops blocking the small redcoat garrison across the York at Gloucester, but Cornwallis planned to fight his way through them.

"So the night of October 16th and early in the morning October 17th," Ranger Williams continued, "they started taking those troops across by boat. They managed to get a thousand across. But again weather intervened. A terrible storm came up and scattered and damaged the boats. Cornwallis now realized that he had no choice but to offer to surrender."

Contemplating Cornwallis's years in America, Lieutenant Colonel "Light-Horse Harry" Lee of Virginia would reflect, "Battle after battle had he fought; climate after climate had he endured; towns had yielded to his mandate, posts were abandoned at his approach; armies were conquered by his prowess . . . But here even he, in the midst of his splendid career, found his conqueror." (The same could be said of Lee's youngest son, Robert E., a great general who would also surrender to Ulysses S. Grant in Virginia eighty-four years later.)

Ranger Williams: "On the morning of October 17th, a drummer came up on the earthworks beating for a parley with an officer beside him waving a handkerchief. Cannonballs were literally bouncing all over the place. And the Americans said if they had not seen the bright red jacket of the officer through all the smoke, they would not have heard that drummer beating for a parley. But when they saw the officer's jacket, the Americans and the French silenced the cannons, and it got quiet for the first time in eight days. They could hear that drummer beating for a parley, and the Americans said it was one of the most incredible sounds they ever heard. Cornwallis sent a message saying he would like a cessation of hostilities for twenty-four hours while he thought about things. Washington knew he was stalling and said, 'You tell him he's got two hours.' Cornwallis knew he had no choice. He sent commissioned officers over to the Moore house, and it was there they spent hours negotiating the terms."

The white clapboard Moore house still stands on the grounds of Colonial National Historical Park. John Laurens represented the Continentals, and Lafayette's in-law the Vicomte de Noailles represented Rochambeau. Cornwallis sent a pair of his underlings, a Major Ross and a Lieutenant Colonel Dundas. The Brits lobbied to perform the ritual of surrender in traditional European military style with their own flags flying and their bands playing an American song as a tribute.

Before the negotiation began, the American and French leadership had held a meeting about what to do regarding the so-called honors of war. The French were willing to grant this tribute and the Americans tended to agree. But Lafayette recalled in his memoirs that he spoke up and reminded them "that the same enemy had required General Lincoln, at the capitulation of Charlestown, to furl the American colours and not to play an English march, insist[ing] strongly on using the same measures with them in retaliation, and obtained that these two precise conditions should be inserted in the capitulation."

Major Ross pointed out to Laurens, "My Lord Cornwallis did not command at Charleston." Which was true. Henry Clinton was the British commander at Charleston who denied the honors of war to General Lincoln and his Continentals, one of whom was the man across from Ross, John Laurens.

Laurens refused to budge. He replied, "It is not the individual that is here considered. It is the nation."

"The British expected to get good terms of surrender," said Ranger Williams, "and the Americans were not about to let them have it. They said, no, you're going to get the same terms of surrender that you gave the American army in Charleston, South Carolina. You're going to march out with your flags down and furled, you'll have to give up all your weapons, and you're all going to be taken as prisoners of war. The Americans were not going to forget how that army had been treated in Charleston. So the British surrendered on those terms, and they didn't like it very much."

Henry Knox wrote to his wife, "They will have the same *honors* as the garrison of Charleston; that is, they will not be permitted to unfurl their colors, or play *Yankee Doodle*."

It's hard to believe that the redcoats not being allowed to play a song with the word "macaroni" in it was, in the context of eighteenth-century European military culture, some sort of bone-deep snub. But from what I can tell, it was met with the same combination of revulsion and indignation I once saw on the face of a Japanese tour guide when I accidentally walked on a tatami mat without taking off my shoes.

And so the official articles of capitulation stipulated, "The garrison of York will march out to a place to be appointed in front of the posts, at two o'clock precisely, with shouldered arms, colours cased, and drums beating a British or German march."

No one recorded what those marches were, though decades later there was an apocryphal and later-debunked story that one of the songs the British played was the on-the-nose "The World Turned Upside Down." The only thing we know for sure is that an American band did strike up "Yankee Doodle" during the surrender ritual, because Lafayette got miffed that the Britons filing up to hand over their weapons refused to look at the Americans, fixing their stares on the French instead. So Lafayette called for a sudden burst of "Yankee Doodle" on the American side as a way of shocking the redcoats into glancing in the patriot victors' direction.

Today, the surrender field is a silent, grassy expanse surrounded by trees maintained by the National Park Service. The gauntlet the British and Hessians had to walk to lay down their arms is marked with a picturesque wooden fence. On the afternoon of October 19, 1781, the French lined up along one side and the Americans lined up a few yards across from them, awaiting the nearly eight thousand defeated troops.

Harry Lee reported, "Every eye was turned, searching for the British commander in chief, anxious to look at that man, heretofore so much the object of their dread. All were disappointed. Cornwallis held himself back from the humiliating scene." Cornwallis, feigning illness, sent his second in command, Lieutenant General Charles O'Hara, to lead the beaten troops in his stead. Pennsylvanian Ebenezer Denny recorded that the losers marched onto the field accompanied by percussionists whose "drums beat as if they did not care how."

O'Hara approached Rochambeau to surrender Cornwallis's sword, but Rochambeau's aide blocked the path, and Rochambeau pointed at Washington across the way. Harry Lee watched as O'Hara "advance[d] up to Washington, asked pardon for his mistake, apologized for the absence of lord Cornwallis, and begged to know his further pleasure. The general feeling his embarrassment, relieved it by referring him with much politeness to general Lincoln." In other words, Washington refused to accept the sword of surrender from Cornwallis's second in command and referred O'Hara to his second, General Lincoln, who then handed back the sword.

Dr. Thacher remarked that the British troops' "mortification could not be concealed. Some of the platoon officers appeared to be exceedingly chagrined . . . many of the soldiers manifested a sullen temper, throwing their arms on the pile with violence, as if determined to render them useless."

The following day, Cornwallis wrote to Clinton, "I have the mortification to inform your Excellency that I have been forced to give up the posts of York and Gloucester, and to surrender the troops under my command, by capitulation, on the 19th instant, as prisoners of war to the combined forces of America and France." Clinton and the British fleet were just then barreling south to come to Cornwallis's rescue. Too late.

Lafayette would no doubt approve of the bombastic name of the town's state-sponsored history museum, the Victory Center.

But I do wonder what Washington would think of it. His orders the day after the surrender set an austere tone, encouraging the troops to commemorate their victory by attending church services with "seriousness of deportment and gratitude of heart."

Lafayette, who would soon sail back to France, celebrated the surrender by penning perky letters home to Vergennes and to his wife. To French prime minister Maurepas, the man who once groaned that Lafayette wanted him to sell all the furniture at Versailles and give the proceeds to the Americans, Lafayette summed up the significance of Yorktown: "The play, sir, is over—and the fifth act has just been closed."

While Lafayette's letters from Yorktown reached France in an unheard-of eighteen days, word of Cornwallis's surrender was slower to reach London. On November 25, Lord George Germain made his way to Downing Street to inform the prime minister, Lord North. North took the news, according to Germain, as if he had just been shot, exclaiming, "O God! It is all over!"

That night Germain was hosting a dinner party at his house, and he decided to keep the bad news about Yorktown to himself. He did, however, mention to his guests that he had heard that French prime minister Maurepas was on his deathbed. One of the guests quipped that it was too bad that Maurepas would die before he found out how the war in America was going to turn out. So Germain decided to spill his guts about Virginia after all, announcing that Maurepas did know who won the war. "The army has surrendered," blurted Germain.

At Yorktown, Ranger Williams announced, "This was the

LAFAYETTE

battle that won the American Revolution. And remember, just six months before this, George Washington had been in such desperation that he had written, 'We are at the end of our tether.' Within six months of Washington writing those desperate words, events remarkably aligned themselves. This was the last major battle of the American Revolution. By now, it had become a world war. You had Spain involved. France involved. The Netherlands involved. Seemed like everybody had something against Great Britain. So, because of that, the peace treaty was going to be very complex and it was going to take two years to negotiate and finalize."

In the Treaty of Paris of 1783, "His Britannic Majesty acknowledges the said United States . . . to be free sovereign and Independent States."

Benjamin Franklin gingerly informed foreign minister Vergennes that the American delegation had worked out a tentative agreement with Britain behind the backs of the French, technically a violation of the Franco-American Treaty of Alliance of '78 that had the soldiers at Valley Forge shouting, "Long live the King of France!" Vergennes lamented, "We shall be but poorly paid for all that we have done for the United States, and for securing to them a national existence." For all their efforts, the French take for helping the Americans wasn't much more than ownership of the disputed island of Tobago.

Ranger Williams concluded her talk at the Yorktown battlefield: "Ladies and gentlemen, you are standing here on very special ground. You are standing with the likes of George Washington, Alexander Hamilton, Lafayette, and Cornwallis.

People from several different **nations** converged on this village of Yorktown to determine the fate of an independent America. And every year on July 4th, what do Americans celebrate? The signing of the Declaration of Independence in 1776, when, after one year of war, America officially declared its independence from Great Britain with a radical document, particularly that second paragraph that began with these famous words, *We hold these truths to be self-evident, that all men are created equal.* Now, we know in America's history we sure have stumbled on that. We have made horrible mistakes, and we've had incredible successes. As a nation, we're still working out what those ideals mean to us. But those would have just been beautiful words on a beautifully written piece of paper if what happened here had not happened."

Following the lead of John Adams, Americans prefer to think of the American Revolution not as an eight-year war but rather as a revolution "effected before the War commenced." We like to believe, as Adams did, that "the Revolution was in the minds and hearts of the people," as opposed to the amputated limbs and bayoneted torsos of Continental and French casualties.

Of course Americans celebrate Independence Day as opposed to Yorktown Day. Who wants to barbecue a hot dog and ponder how we owe our independence to the French navy? Who wants to twirl sparklers and dwell on how the French government's expenditures in America contributed to the bankruptcy that sparked the French Revolution that would send Rochambeau to prison, Lafayette into exile (then prison), and our benefactor His Most Christian Majesty Louis XVI to the guillotine.

That said, Americans finding themselves in Paris on the Fourth of July should swing by Picpus Cemetery, where Lafayette is buried under dirt from Bunker Hill. There is an emotional annual ceremony there, in which representatives of the French and American governments and military join the descendants of Lafayette, along with anyone else who cares, to witness the American flag flying over Lafayette's grave being swapped out for a fresh Stars and Stripes. I went with my friend Steven, a dual citizen of France and the United States, who confessed to being touched by "the most patriotic event I have ever attended."

Around the corner from the Place de la Nation, where a guillotine cranked out corpses at a quick clip during the Terror, Picpus was established as a private cemetery, partly through the efforts of Lafayette's wife, Adrienne. The bodies of her mother and sister were discarded there, along with the thirteen hundred beheaded nobles, commoners, clergymen, and nuns whom the radicals tossed into the mass graves dug on the site. Among the victims lies the great chemist Antoine Lavoisier, who discovered and named oxygen and hydrogen. "It took them only an instant to cut off that head," a mathematician remarked on Lavoisier's execution, "but France may not produce another like it in a century."

Adrienne, imprisoned in Paris during the Terror after Austrians captured Lafayette, was spared the guillotine only by the lobbying of the U.S. minister to France, the future president James Monroe, and his wife, Elizabeth. In his Fourth of July speech at Lafayette's grave, Mark Taplin, the U.S. embassy's deputy chief of mission, recalled, "As Lafayette faced years of imprisonment in an Austrian dungeon, his family the prospect of starvation . . . Elizabeth Monroe bravely visited Lafayette's wife, in prison, and the Monroes secured her and her daughter passports so they could join Lafayette in Austria." (Georges Washington Lafayette escaped unscathed to the United States, where he attended Harvard and lived for a time with his namesake's family at Mount Vernon.)

Taplin proclaimed, "Lafayette, in turn, never relented in his devotion to America, even for all her faults. He acknowledged to his American hosts on his triumphal return tour to the U.S. that there was 'much to deplore' in the South's practice of slavery. But there was still much to admire there, he quickly added. Lafayette lifted his glass at one reception to toast 'the perpetual union of the United States,' adding, 'it has always saved us in time of storm; one day it will save the world.'"

Whether or not the United States has saved the world, it did save France a time or two. When the American Expeditionary Forces commanded by General John J. Pershing came to the aid of France during World War I, they marched into Paris on July 4, 1917, heading straight for Picpus Cemetery. Colonel Charles E. Stanton, whose uncle had been Abraham Lincoln's secretary of war, addressed the French people while standing before Lafayette's tomb. "America has joined forces with the Allied Powers," he said, "and what we have of blood and treasure are yours. Therefore it is that with loving pride we drape the colors in tribute of respect to this citizen of your great republic.

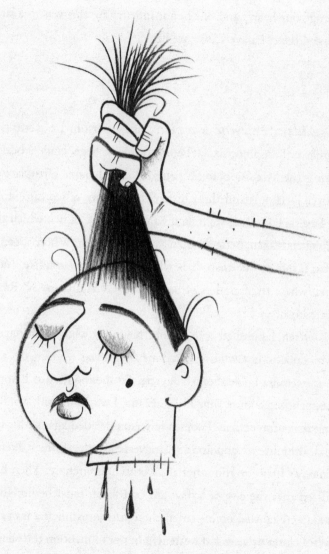

KING LOUIS XVI

And here and now, in the presence of the illustrious dead, we pledge our hearts and our honor in carrying this war to a successful issue. Lafayette, we are here."

Nowadays, Lafayette is a place, not a person. Lafayette is a boulevard in Phoenix, a Pennsylvania college, and a bridge across the Mississippi in St. Paul. It's the Alabama birthplace of boxer Joe Louis and three different towns in Wisconsin—four if Fayette counts. If so, then it's also Fayette County, which the Chicken Ranch, better known as the Best Little Whorehouse in Texas, put on the map. It is without question Lafayette, Indiana, where the founders of both C-SPAN and Guns N' Roses were born.

When I bumped into an old neighbor whilst visiting my Montana hometown, she asked me what I was working on, and I answered a book about Lafayette. So she inquired if I would be spending a lot of time in Louisiana. I was confused, wondering if she forgot that Thomas Jefferson decided against his initial impulse of appointing Lafayette as the former French colony's first governor after the Louisiana Purchase. Then I realized that the city of Lafayette, Louisiana, must be her go-to Lafayette-labeled noun—even though from Montana it's actually a closer drive to Lafayette, Utah, not to mention the ones in Oregon, California, Kansas, and Colorado. So I explained that I meant Lafayette the French teenager who crossed the Atlantic on his own dime to volunteer to fight with George Washington in the Revolutionary War. Therefore, I said, I was more likely to visit Pennsylvania, where he got shot. She nevertheless professed her fondness for zydeco.

This encounter aroused such indignation in my breast that I moralized upon the instability of human glory and the evanescence of many other things. No, wait, that's what Herman Melville did in 1870 when a random stranger in a cigar store had never heard of his Revolutionary War–hero grandfather. When I found out my old neighbor had never heard of my Revolutionary War–hero protagonist, I went and got a taco with my sister. Still, it does seem eerie how one day in 1824 two-thirds of the population of New York City was lining up to wave hello to Lafayette and nineteen decades go by and all that's left of his memory is the name of a Cajun college town.

Thanks to the nationwide euphoria over the elderly Lafayette's return tour of the United States, countless American streets, parks, cities, counties, schools, warships, horses, and babies bear his name. The long list includes Scientology founder Lafayette Ronald "L. Ron" Hubbard and my Arkansas-born great-great-uncle Lafayette Hinds, who went by "Fate" for short.

The most meaningful namesake by far is Lafayette Square, across the street from the White House. Also known as Lafayette Park, this is the nation's capital of protest, the place where we the people gather together to yell at our presidents.

In each corner of this seven-acre park stands a statue of four of the most revered European officers who served in the Revolutionary War: Lafayette, Rochambeau, Steuben, and Thaddeus Kosciuszko, the Polish engineer whose defensive works contributed to the Continental Army's victory at Saratoga. Or as one of the anti-nuclear protesters who have kept up a continual peace vigil in the park since 1981 referred to the warrior statues when I chatted with her the last time I visited the park, "goons with guns."

While I am baffled by the off-topic inclusion of an equestrian statue of President Andrew Jackson lording over the center of a square honoring the contributions of foreign fighters, I do approve of the bronze Jackson's gesture of tipping his hat, evoking Walt Whitman's explanation for the "genius" of the American people as "the President's taking off his hat to them and not they to him."

Lafayette Park has hosted civil rights activists picketing Lyndon Johnson to send federal troops to protect their comrades in Alabama after the "Bloody Sunday" march in Selma, various tent cities called "Reaganville" that homeless advocates erected throughout the 1980s, and the demonstrators against the Persian Gulf War, who, George H. W. Bush once complained to *Parade* magazine, were "beating those damn drums in front of the White House when I was trying to have dinner."

Of all the rallies, sit-ins, and acts of civil disobedience staged at Lafayette Square over the decades, perhaps the one that Americans should be the most proud of is the gathering the Ku Klux Klan convened there in 1982. The three dozen or so white supremacist dunderheads who showed up to demonstrate were provided police protection against the hordes of agitated counterprotesters pouring into the capital to demonstrate against their demonstration. Freedom of expression truly exists only when a society's most repugnant nitwits are allowed to spew their nonsense in public. In Lafayette Park distasteful speech is literally permitted, with permits issued by the National Park Service, the federal agency managing the site.

Numerous court cases have been filed to keep the Secret Service or the Department of the Interior from closing or limiting protesters' access to Lafayette Square because of concerns for the safety of the president (or the park's foliage). In 1974, after nearly a decade of litigation pursued by a coalition of Quakers, Vietnam War protesters, and both Jews for Urban Justice and the Action Committee on American-Arab Relations, the District of Columbia Circuit of the U.S. Court of Appeals upheld a ruling against discrimination in the issuing of permits and chastised the National Park Service's periodic attempts to curb demonstrations in Lafayette Square because "use of parks for public assembly and airing of opinions is historic in our democratic society, and one of its cardinal values." Regarding the president's safety, Judge Harold Leventhal opined that in a democracy, "the President cannot be kept in a steel room away from the public."

Among the scores of protests held in Lafayette Park during the administration of Barack Obama, environmentalists have sounded off against genetically modified foods and the construction of a new oil pipeline; Muslims have prayed en masse to protest Israel's incursion in the Gaza Strip; immigration reformers have denounced the president's deportation policies; members of the Tea Party have commemorated Tax Day carrying signs proclaiming, "Give me liberty . . . NOT DEBT"; and

Students to Free Tibet have picketed the visiting Chinese president with signs marked, "Tibet is not a part of China."

If those Tibetans held up that same placard calling for Tibetan independence in China and/or Tibet, they would undoubtedly be arrested and charged with "splittism," the Chinese government's name for separatist outbursts it deems a threat to national harmony. In Lafayette Square, separatist outbursts are just called Tuesday—or Wednesday, Thursday, etc.

It would please Lafayette that the pleasant patch of grass bearing his name is where all sorts of splittists, foreign and domestic, routinely air their grievances. After all, the only reason there's a statue of him staring at the White House is because as a teenager he defied his father-in-law's edict to settle into a boring job at the French court, explaining afterward, "I did not hesitate to be disagreeable to preserve my independence."

The tradition of protest in Lafayette Park dates back to the World War I era, when the disagreeable dames in the National Woman's Party picketed President Woodrow Wilson for years, demanding his support in their campaign to pass a constitutional amendment guaranteeing women the right to vote. Which sounds so upstanding. It wasn't. The abuse those women suffered in the name of suffrage is one of American history's more upsetting episodes. Daring to demand, during wartime, the basic and sacred right to vote, the NWP's "Silent Sentinels" picketing Wilson were beaten by male passersby as the police looked on without coming to the women's aid, arrested repeatedly for "blocking traffic," and jailed in an unsanitary prison workhouse. When Alice Paul, the NWP's incarcerated Quaker leader, refused to eat her hellhole prison's vermin-infested food, authorities answered her hunger strike by strapping her down and ramming a tube funneling raw eggs down her throat. All because the NWP protesters would stand in front of the White House or the statue of Lafayette and burn President Wilson's war speeches about how "the world must be made safe for democracy" when the only American women who had the right to vote were the ones living in the handful of mostly Western states where it was legal. The NWP's mission was the passage of the Susan B. Anthony Amendment ensuring women's suffrage at the national level. The bill was named for the suffragist who crashed the centennial celebration at Independence Hall on July 4, 1876, proclaiming, "We ask that all the civil and political rights that belong to citizens of the United States, be guaranteed to us and our daughters forever."

Before the Anthony Amendment was renamed the Nineteenth and ratified in 1920, Evelyn Wotherspoon Wainwright of the National Woman's Party walked up to the statue of Lafayette in Lafayette Square on September 16, 1918, and gave a speech. Married to a naval commander who happened to be Benjamin Franklin's great-great-grandson, Wainwright prayed to the graven image of Lafayette, since neither the president nor Congress seemed to be listening.

"We, the women of the United States," she told the bronze Lafayette, "denied the liberty which you helped to gain, and for which we have asked in vain for sixty years, turn to you to plead for us. Speak, Lafayette, dead these hundred years but still living in the hearts of the American people."

She beseeched the inanimate Frenchman, "Let that outstretched hand of yours pointing to the White House recall to him"—President Wilson—"his words and promises, his trumpet call for all of us, to see that the world is made safe for democracy. As our army now in France spoke to you there, saying here we are to help your country fight for liberty, will you not speak here and now for us, a little band with no army, no power but justice and right, no strength but in our Constitution and in the Declaration of Independence; and win a great victory again in this country by giving us the opportunity we ask—to be heard through the Susan B. Anthony amendment."

She then echoed the words uttered by the American officer in Paris on July 4, 1917. "Lafayette," she said, "we are here!"

BIBLIOGRAPHY

Adams, Charles Francis, ed. *Familiar Letters of John Adams and His Wife Abigail Adams During the Revolution with a Memoir of Mrs. Adams.* New York: Hurd and Houghton, 1876.

———. *The Works of John Adams.* Boston: Little, Brown & Co., 1850–56.

———. *Letters of John Adams, Addressed to His Wife.* Boston: Freeman and Bolles, 1841.

Adams, William Howard. *The Paris Years of Thomas Jefferson.* New Haven: Yale University Press, 1997.

Arendt, Hannah. *On Revolution.* New York: Penguin Books, 1977.

Bancroft, George. *History of the United States from the Discovery of the Continent.* Boston: Little, Brown & Co., 1834–37.

Brown, Victoria Bissell. "Did Woodrow Wilson's Gender Politics Matter?" In *Reconsidering Woodrow Wilson: Progressivism, Internationalism, War, and Peace.* Edited by John Milton Cooper, Jr. Baltimore: Johns Hopkins University Press, 2008.

Burrows, Edwin G. *Forgotten Patriots: The Untold Story of American Patriots During the Revolutionary War.* New York: Basic Books, 2008.

Carbone, Gerald M. *Nathanael Greene: A Biography of the American Revolution.* New York: Palgrave Macmillan, 2008.

Carp, E. Wayne. *To Starve the Army at Pleasure: Continental Army Administration and American Political Culture, 1775–1783.* Chapel Hill: University of North Carolina Press, 1984.

Cash, Arthur. *John Wilkes: The Scandalous Father of Civil Liberties.* New Haven: Yale University Press, 2007.

Chernow, Ron. *Washington: A Life.* New York: Penguin Books, 2010.

Clary, David A. *Adopted Son: Washington, Lafayette, and the Friendship That Saved the Revolution.* New York: Bantam, 2007.

Clinton, Henry. *The Narrative of Lieutenant-General Sir Henry Clinton, K.B., Relative to His Conduct During Part of His Command of the King's Troops in North America: Particularly to That Which Respects the Unfortunate Issue of the Campaign in 1781.* London: John Debrett, 1785.

Cornwallis, Charles. *An Answer to That Part of the Narrative of Lt. General Sir Henry Clinton, K.B.* London: John Debrett, 1783.

Denny, Ebenezer. *Military Journal of Major Ebenezer Denny, an Officer in the Revolutionary and Indian Wars.* Philadelphia: Historical Society of Pennsylvania, 1859.

Dorsey, Peter A. *Common Bondage: Slavery as Metaphor in Revolutionary America.* Knoxville: University of Tennessee Press, 2009.

Doyle, Joseph Beatty. *Frederick William von Steuben and the American Revolution: Aide to Washington and Inspector General of the Army.* Steubenville, OH: H. C. Cook Co., 1913.

Drake, Francis Samuel. *Life and Correspondence of Henry Knox, Major General in the American Revolutionary Army.* Boston: Samuel G. Drake, 1873.

Duer, William A., ed. *Memoirs, Correspondence and Manuscripts of General Lafayette, Published by His Family.* New York: 1837.

Dull, Jonathan R. *A Diplomatic History of the American Revolution.* New Haven: Yale University Press, 1985.

Ellis, Joseph J. *American Sphinx: The Character of Thomas Jefferson.* New York: Random House, 1996.

———. *His Excellency: George Washington.* New York: Alfred A. Knopf, 2004.

Fitzpatrick, John C., ed. *The Writings of George Washington.* Washington, DC: Government Printing Office, 1931–44.

Fleming, Thomas J. *Beat the Last Drum.* New York: St. Martin's Press, 1963.

Ford, Paul Leicester. "Dr. Rush and General Washington." *Atlantic Monthly,* May 1895.

Gaines, James R. *For Liberty and Glory: Washington, Lafayette, and Their Revolutions.* New York: W. W. Norton, 2007.

Giunta, Mary A., with J. Dane Hartgrove, eds. *Documents of the Emerging Nation: U.S. Foreign Relations, 1775–1789.* Wilmington, DE: Scholarly Resources, 1998.

Golway, Terry. *Washington's General: Nathanael Greene and the Triumph of the American Revolution.* New York: Henry Holt, 2005.

Gordon, David, ed. *The Turgot Collection: Writings, Speeches, and Letters of Anne Robert Jacques Turgot, Baron de Laune.* Auburn, AL: Ludwig von Mises Institute, 2011.

Grainger, John D. *The Battle of Yorktown 1781: A Reassessment.* Rochester, NY: Boydell Press, 2005.

Greene, Jerome. *The Guns of Independence: The Siege of Yorktown, 1781.* New York: Savas Beatie, 2005.

Handler, Richard, and Eric Gable. *New History in an Old Museum: Creating the Past at Colonial Williamsburg.* Durham, NC: Duke University Press, 1997.

Harris, Michael. *Brandywine: A Military History of the Battle That Lost Philadelphia but Saved America, September 11, 1777.* El Dorado Hills, CA: Savas Beatie, 2014.

Isaacson, Walter. *Benjamin Franklin: An American Life.* New York: Simon & Schuster, 2004.

Jefferson, Thomas. *Thomas Jefferson: A Chronology of His Thoughts.* Edited by Jerry Holmes. Lanham, MD: Rowman & Littlefield, 2002.

Jones, Colin. *The Cambridge Illustrated History of France.* Cambridge, UK: Cambridge University Press, 1994.

Kapp, Friedrich. *The Life of Frederick William von Steuben, Major General in the Revolutionary Army.* New York: Mason Bros., 1859.

Ketchum, Richard M. *Victory at Yorktown:*

The Campaign That Won the Revolution. New York: Henry Holt, 2004.

Lafayette, Marquis de, and Thomas Jefferson. *The Letters of Lafayette and Jefferson.* Introduction and notes by Gilbert Chinard. Baltimore: Johns Hopkins Press, 1929.

Lane, Jason. *General and Madame de Lafayette: Partners in Liberty's Cause in the American and French Revolutions.* Lanham, MD: Taylor Trade Publishing, 2003.

Laurens, Henry. *The Papers of Henry Laurens: November 1, 1777–March 15, 1778.* Columbia, SC: University of South Carolina Press, 1990.

Lengel, Edward G. *General George Washington: A Military Life.* New York: Random House, 2005.

Lesser, Charles H., ed. *The Sinews of Independence: Monthly Strength Reports of the Continental Army.* Chicago: University of Chicago Press, 1976.

Levasseur, Auguste. *Lafayette in America in 1824 and 1825: Journal of a Voyage to the United States.* Translated by Alan Hoffman. Manchester, NH: Lafayette Press, 2006.

Lever, Maurice. *Beaumarchais: A Biography.* Translated by Susan Emanuel. New York: Farrar, Straus & Giroux, 2009.

Lockhart, Paul. *The Drillmaster of Valley Forge: The Baron de Steuben and the Making of the American Army.* New York: Smithsonian Books, 2008.

Luvaas, Jay, ed. and trans. *Frederick the Great on the Art of War.* New York: Da Capo Press, 1999.

Manca, Joseph. *George Washington's Eye: Landscape, Architecture, and Design at Mount Vernon.* Baltimore: Johns Hopkins University Press, 2012.

Martin, Joseph Plumb. *A Narrative of a Revolutionary Soldier: Some of the Adventures, Misgivings, and Sufferings of Joseph Plumb Martin.* New York: Signet Classic, 2001.

McBurney, Christian. *The Rhode Island Campaign: The First French and American Operation in the Revolutionary War.* Yardley, PA: Westholme, 2011.

McCullough, David. *John Adams.* New York: Simon & Schuster, 2001.

McGuire, Thomas J. *The Philadelphia Campaign: Brandywine and the Fall of Philadelphia.* Mechanicsburg, PA: Stackpole Books, 2006.

Morgan, Edmund S. *The Genius of George Washington.* Washington, DC: Society of the Cincinnati, 1980.

Morgan, George. *The True Lafayette.* Philadelphia: J. B. Lippincott, 1919.

Morton, Brian N., and Donald C. Spinelli. *Beaumarchais and the American Revolution.* Lanham, MD: Lexington Press, 2001.

Murphy, Orville T. "The Battle of Germantown and the Franco-American Alliance of 1778." *Pennsylvania Magazine of History and Biography,* January 1958.

———. *Charles Gravier, Comte de Vergennes: French Diplomacy in the Age of Revolution, 1719–1787.* Albany: State University of New York Press, 1982.

Nelson, Craig. *Thomas Paine: Enlightenment, Revolution, and the Birth of Modern Nations.* New York: Viking, 2006.

O'Shaughnessy, Andrew Jackson. *The Men Who Lost America: British Leadership, the American Revolution and the Fate of Empire.* New Haven: Yale University Press, 2013.

Parker, Hersel. *Herman Melville: A Biography, volume 1: 1819–1851.* Baltimore: The Johns Hopkins University Press, 1996.

Perkins, James Breck. *France in the American Revolution.* New York: Houghton Mifflin, 1911.

Prowell, George R. *Continental Congress at York, Pennsylvania, and York County in the Revolution.* York, PA: York Printing Co., 1914.

Puls, Mark. *Henry Knox: Visionary General of the American Revolution.* New York: Palgrave Macmillan, 2008.

Remini, Robert V. *Andrew Jackson: The Course of American Democracy, 1833–1845*. New York: Harper & Row, 1984.

Rhodehamel, John, ed. *The American Revolution: Writings from the War of Independence*. New York: Library of America, 2001.

Russell, David Lee. *The American Revolution in the Southern Colonies*. Jefferson, NC, and London: McFarland, 2000.

Schama, Simon. *Citizens: A Chronicle of the French Revolution*. New York: Random House, 1989.

Schiff, Stacy. *A Great Improvisation: Franklin, France, and the Birth of America*. New York: Henry Holt, 2005.

Selesky, Harold E. *A Demographic Survey of the Continental Army That Wintered at Valley Forge, Pennsylvania, 1777–1778*. Washington, DC: U.S. Government Printing Office, 1988.

Shilts, Randy. *Conduct Unbecoming: Gays and Lesbians in the U.S. Military*. New York: St. Martin's Press, 1993.

Sparks, Jared. *The Life of Washington*. Boston: Tappan & Dennet, 1843.

———. *The Writings of George Washington*. Boston: Tappan & Dennet, 1834–37.

Stein, Susan R. *The Worlds of Thomas Jefferson at Monticello*. New York: Harry N. Abrams, 1993.

Stoll, Ira. *Samuel Adams: A Life*. New York: Free Press, 2008.

Thacher, James. *A Military Journal During the American Revolutionary War*. Boston: Richardson & Lord, 1823.

Unger, Harlow Giles. *Improbable Patriot: The Secret History of Monsieur de Beaumarchais, the French Playwright Who Saved the American Revolution*. Lebanon, NH: University Press of New England, 2011.

———. *Lafayette*. Hoboken, NJ: John Wiley & Sons, 2002.

United States Library of Congress. *A Century of Lawmaking for a New Nation: U.S. Congressional Documents and Debates, 1774–1875*. http://memory.loc.gov/ammem/amlaw/.

von Steuben, Baron Frederick William. *Baron Von Steuben's Revolutionary War Drill Manual: A Facsimile Reprint of the 1794 Edition*. Mineola, NY: Dover Publications, 1985.

Whiteley, Peter. *Lord North: The Prime Minister Who Lost America*. London: Hambledon Press, 1996.

Whitridge, Arnold. *Rochambeau*. New York: Macmillan, 1965.

Wood, Gordon S. *The Radicalism of the American Revolution*. New York: Alfred A. Knopf, 1992.

ACKNOWLEDGMENTS

I would like to thank my longtime, long-suffering editor, publisher, and friend, Geoffrey Kloske of Riverhead Books. Also at Riverhead, Caty Gordon, Maureen Klier, Lauren Kolm, Helen Yentus, Lisa D'Agostino, Madeline McIntosh, Susan Petersen Kennedy, and Jynne Martin pitched in. Much gratitude to David Levinthal for his cover photograph and Teddy Newton for his illustrations. At Simon and Schuster Audio, Elisa Shokoff was dreamy per usual and Mike Noble was no slouch. At Steven Barclay Agency, Steven Barclay, Sara Bixler, Kathryn Barcos, and Eliza Fischer were as thoughtful as they were organized, which is saying something. I also appreciate Ted Thompson's backup, Jaime Wolf's lawyering, Gabe Taurman's interview transcriptions, and David Sedaris and Hugh Hamrick's hospitality in Paris. Shout-out to Ira Glass for editing my piece on

Lafayette's return to America in 1824 for *This American Life*. I am especially grateful to my traveling companions Jonathan Sherman, Wesley Stace, Amy Vowell, and Owen Brooker.

Thanks also to Ranger Linda Williams at Colonial National Historical Park; Amy Atticks, Anna Berkes, Peggy Cornett, Andrea Gray, Ellen Hickman, Andrew Jackson O'Shaughnessy, and Susan Stein at Monticello; Susan Schoelwer and Mary Thompson at Mount Vernon; Jim Bradley, Samantha Lacher, and Mark Schneider at Colonial Williamsburg; Xavier Comte at Conseil Général Haute-Loire; and Philip Breeden, Christopher Palmer, and Mark Taplin at the United States embassy in Paris.

Additional help, information, advice, and cheer provided by: J. J. Abrams, Barbara Barclay, Garth Bixler, Eric Bogosian, Peter Carlin, Gilbert de Chambrun, René de Chambrun, Thibault de Chambrun, Katherine Fletcher, Will Garrison at Arrowhead, Michael Giacchino, Daniel Handler, John Hodgman, Hayley Chouinard, Nick Hornby, Lisa Leingang, Tom Levenson, Seth Mnookin, John Petrizzo, Kate Porterfield, Jon Ronson, Alexandra Shiva, Abbey Stace, Travis Tonn, Janie Vowell, Pat Vowell, and Stu Zicherman.

Sarah Vowell is an American original. With her wit, wisdom, and unerring sense of history, politics, and humor, she tells stories of our country's past—the good, the bad, and the ugly. In her inimitable, wry style, history has never been so troubling, so alive, or so funny.

"Sarah Vowell is a Madonna of Americana."

—*Los Angeles Times*

"I love Sarah Vowell's writing—it's smart, funny, soulful, even educational." —**Nick Hornby**

"Vowell makes an excellent traveling companion, what with her rare combination of erudition and cheek."

—Bruce Handy, *The New York Times Book Review*

by Bennett Miller

America views itself as a Puritan nation, but Sarah Vowell investigates what that means—and what it should mean.

What was this great political enterprise all about? Who were these people who are considered the philosophical, spiritual, and moral ancestors of our nation? What Vowell discovers is something far different from what their uptight shoe-buckles-and-corn reputation might suggest. The people she finds are highly literate, deeply principled, and surprisingly feisty while engaged in pamphlet feuds, witty courtroom dramas, and bloody vengeance.

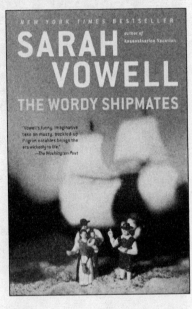

The Wordy Shipmates is rich in historical fact, humorous insight, and social commentary by one of America's most celebrated voices. Thou shalt enjoy it.

Featuring a cast of beguiling, appalling, and tragic characters, including sugar barons, con men, brother-husbands, Theodore Roosevelt, and the last Hawaiian queen...

Sarah Vowell explores the Americanization of Hawaii—from the arrival of New England missionaries in 1820 to the events leading up to American annexation in 1898.

With her wry insights and reporting, Vowell explores the odd, emblematic, and exceptional history of the fiftieth state and, in so doing, finds America, warts and all.

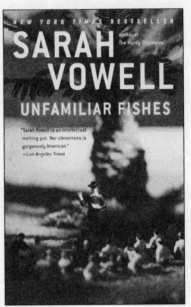

"A tour de force...Vowell is a national treasure, exploring the depths of what it means to be American." —*The Boston Globe*

"Sarah Vowell is an intellectual melting pot. Her cleverness is gorgeously American." —*Los Angeles Times*